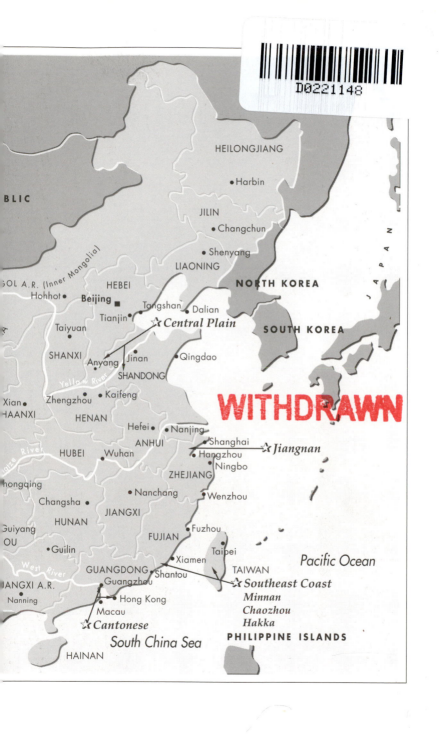

HEILONGJIANG

• Harbin

JILIN

• Changchun

• Shenyang

LIAONING

NORTH KOREA

HEBEI

Hohhot •

GOL A.R. (Inner Mongolia)

**Beijing** ■

Tangshan • • Dalian

Tianjin •

☆ *Central Plain*

SOUTH KOREA

Taiyuan

SHANXI

Anyang • Jinan

• Qingdao

SHANDONG

Yellow River

Xian •

HAANXI

Zhengzhou • • Kaifeng

HENAN

**WITHDRAWN**

Hefei • • Nanjing

ANHUI

HUBEI Wuhan •

• Shanghai ☆ *Jiangnan*

• Hangzhou

Ningbo

Yangtze River

hongqing

ZHEJIANG

Changsha •

• Nanchang

• Wenzhou

HUNAN

JIANGXI

Guiyang

OU

• Guilin

FUJIAN

• Fuzhou

• Xiamen

Taipei

West River

GUANGDONG Shantou

TAIWAN

Pacific Ocean

ANGXI A.R.

Guangzhou

☆ *Southeast Coast*

Nanning •

• Hong Kong

*Minnan*

Macau

*Chaozhou*

☆ *Cantonese*

*Hakka*

*South China Sea*

PHILIPPINE ISLANDS

HAINAN

BLIC

J A P A N

D0221148

# Chinese Musical Instruments

# TITLES IN THE SERIES

Series Editors, China Titles:
NIGEL CAMERON, SYLVIA FRASER-LU

# Chinese Musical Instruments

ALAN R. THRASHER

OXFORD
UNIVERSITY PRESS

# OXFORD
UNIVERSITY PRESS

Oxford University Press is a department of the University of Oxford.
It furthers the University's objective of excellence in research, scholarship,
and education by publishing worldwide in

Oxford New York

Athens Auckland Bangkok Bogotá Buenos Aires Calcutta
Cape Town Chennai Dar es Salaam Delhi Florence Hong Kong Istanbul
Karachi Kuala Lumpur Madrid Melbourne Mexico City Mumbai
Nairobi Paris São Paulo Shanghai Singapore Taipei Tokyo Toronto Warsaw

with associated companies in Berlin Ibadan

Oxford is a registered trade mark of Oxford University Press

Published in the United States
by Oxford University Press Inc., New York

© Oxford University Press 2000

First published 2000
This impression (lowest digit)
1 3 5 7 9 10 8 6 4 2

All rights reserved. No part of this publication may be reproduced,
stored in a retrieval system, or transmitted, in any form or by any means,
without the prior permission in writing of Oxford University Press,
or as expressly permitted by Law, or under terms agreed with the appropriate
reprographics rights organization. Enquiries concerning reproduction
outside the scope of the above should be sent to the Rights Department,
Oxford University Press, at the address below

You must not circulate this book in any other binding or cover
and you must impose the same condition on any acquirer

British Library Cataloguing in Publication Data
available

Library of Congress Cataloging-in-Publication Data
available

ISBN 019-590777-9

Printed in Hong Kong
Published by Oxford University Press (China) Ltd
18th Floor, Warwick House East, Taikoo Place, 979 King's Road, Quarry Bay
Hong Kong

# Contents

To my mother Grace,
For her unfailing love and encouragement

# Preface

SOON AFTER THE fifteenth century BC, when prognosticators employed by the Shang kings scratched questions and answers onto cow bones and tortoise shells (the so-called 'oracle bones'), nearly a dozen musical instruments were named—drums of different kinds, resonant stone chimes, panpipes, and others. So important were these instruments in ritual ceremonies, that the classic texts of the Zhou period (eleventh to third centuries BC) cited close to three dozen names, often with some detail as to construction, performance, and function. Indeed, specimens of most have actually been found. Examination of the ancient heritage with a focus on the ritual instruments dominates the first chapter of this book. One of these instruments, the *qin* zither, proved to have musical potential far beyond the world of court ritual. Adopted by the literati class for its subtlety in musical expression, the *qin* very early achieved the high status of one of the classical arts (together with calligraphy and poetry). The entire second chapter is therefore given to the development of this one instrument.

Most musical instruments in common practice today were introduced into China during and following the Han dynasty (206 BC–AD 220), when numerous ideas and artefacts arrived from India and Central Asia with the flow of Buddhism. The earliest of the musical instruments dating to this period are prototypes of the *pipa* lute and *dizi* flute. At the close of the Tang dynasty (618–907), *erhu*-type fiddles emerged, followed by many others during subsequent dynasties. This extraordinary history, extending over a period of two millennia, is exceptionally well documented in imperial music treatises, dynastic histories, period artwork, and archaeological finds. Chinese scholars at the Music Research

Institute in Beijing have spent several decades researching these developments, and at present the monumental series *Zhongguo Yinyue Wenwu Daxi* (Compendium of Chinese Musical Relics) is being published, one volume per province, in a coordinated effort to detail this visual evidence. Within the scope of the present small volume, however, no more than a chapter can be given to historical trends.

It may seem ironic that these introduced instruments, most of which were associated with 'barbarian' peoples, would become so widely accepted in China, some such as the *pipa* emerging as quasi-classical traditions. But the indigenous instruments, with few exceptions, were reserved for ritual usage in the courts. Instruments brought in from outside became popular, forming the core of what I will call the 'common-practice' tradition. This tradition, however, exists in as many variations as there are Chinese regions. In dealing with this diversity, I will follow Chinese musicologists' (sometimes problematic) division of instrumental ensemble music into two broad types: *sizhu* ('silk-bamboo'), essentially a type of chamber music utilizing stringed instruments and bamboo flutes; and *chuida* ('blowing-hitting'), a ritual tradition performed at funerals and calendrical ceremonies, utilizing louder double-reed instruments and cymbals, gongs, and drums. Each broad type is given a chapter. Finally, a very brief postscript will bring the reader up to date on some of the basic changes instruments have undergone during the twentieth century.

This book focuses primarily upon the mainstream instruments of the Han Chinese, the dominant population of China. Instruments are first presented within their social contexts and then described as functional components of the various ensemble types. While basic descriptions are given for most common-practice instruments, my orientation is upon socio-functional contexts, roles within Chinese society, and meanings within the Confucian world view. The whole of present-day China, with all its diversity, cannot be represented in a book of this length. The more than four dozen 'national minorities' living just inside the borders of China clearly maintain musical traditions which are no less important. But these are so numerous they deserve separate treatment; they will not be examined in this volume. Similarly, the more specialized instruments which serve to accompany vocal music (such as traditional opera) must also be reserved for another study.

I wish to express my sincere gratitude to the following people for the assistance they have given at different stages: to Huang Jinpei, Li Minxiong, and Du Yaxiong for guiding my understanding of the local musical traditions of South China, Central-eastern China, and North China respectively, essentially providing the cultural backgrounds against which these instruments can be seen; to Chuang Pen-li for his many insights into the Confucian ritual tradition as practiced in Taiwan; and to Liu Dongsheng and Wu Zhao, the two most active scholars in documenting musical instrument history, for lengthy discussions on recent discoveries and discrepancies between written accounts and preserved artefacts.

I also acknowledge a generous Humanities and Social Sciences grant, awarded by the University of British Columbia, which enabled me to travel to Taipei and Beijing to conduct research at the major museums and instrument collections. Finally, I could not have completed this book without the artistic skills of Cheryl Fan, who spent part of one summer clarifying the details of faded historic line drawings and for providing additional sketches, and the editorial assistance of my wife, Mary Weller, whose many thoughtful comments have been incorporated into the text.

**A Note on Pronunciation**

Several consonants in the *pinyin* spelling system are given unusual linguistic values.

Q is pronounced as 'ch' (e.g. *qin* [zither] is sounded as 'chin'; *qudi* [flute] as 'chü-di').

X is essentially pronounced as 's', though articulated with a forward 'h' sound (e.g. *xun* [flute] as 'hsün'; *xiao* [flute] as 'hsiao').

Z is pronounced as 'dz' (e.g. *dizi* [flute] as 'di-dz').

ZH is pronounced as 'j' (e.g. *zheng* [zither] as 'jeng'; *zhong* [bell] as 'jung').

# 1

# The Ancient Heritage

THE PRACTICE OF burying material possessions with kings and emperors was common in ancient China. Numerous tombs throughout North and Central China have been found during the twentieth century, yielding treasure troves of material culture—ritual vessels, weapons, musical instruments, and even the remains of servants and dancers. It is not so surprising that instruments constructed of clay, stone, or bronze might be found after several thousand years in the ground. But how zithers with silk strings and flutes of bamboo could possibly survive nature's recycling programme for more than a few centuries is quite extraordinary.

The oldest instruments found to date are flutes made from bird or animal bones, with two or more fingerholes, unearthed from sites in North China and dating to between c.6000 and 5000 BC. The most remarkable specimen is constructed from the wing bone of a crane (Plate 1), with seven carefully spaced and meticulously drilled fingerholes (plus a smaller eighth hole near the bottom). This, and others like it, are unnotched at their blowing ends (unlike the end-blown Chinese *xiao*) and presumably held in performance at an oblique angle (perhaps similar to the West Asian *nay* flute). In addition, numerous one- and two-hole clay flutes dating from c.4000 BC (and later) have been found in Shanxi province and other areas. Ball-shaped, egg-shaped, and even fish-shaped, these globular flutes are thought to be prototypes of the *xun* (described below). More unusual among the pre-Shang finds are the resonating stones dating from c.2000 BC, rough lithophones chipped from limestone or other resonant rock. These are believed to be prototypes

1

of the ritually important *qing* stone chimes (described below).[1]

## Shang Finds and the Bone Inscriptions

The most significant finds of Shang-dynasty instruments (*c.*16th to 11th centuries BC) have been unearthed in northern Henan province, particularly at sites near the town of Anyang. Shang instruments, most dating to about the twelfth century BC, display remarkable sophistication in form and design. These include: small egg-shaped globular flutes (*xun*) of bone or baked clay, with three fingerholes in front, two thumbholes in back, and blowhole at the top; stone chimes (*qing*) in triangular, rectangular, and other shapes, both single pieces and in sets of three, made from highly polished slabs of limestone or marble; bronze bells without clappers (*nao*), short and broad in profile, designed to be held mouth upward and struck with a beater;[2] small bronze bells with clappers (*ling*), somewhat triangular in shape, suspended mouth downward by loops and shaken; barrel-shaped drums (*gu*), of which the only surviving examples are instruments now called 'bronze drums' (*tonggu*), made entirely of bronze (including the drumheads) and resting horizontally on four legs. This group of instruments, together with panpipes and a few others, would become the core of the Chinese ritual ensemble.

Shang design is spectacular. On many instruments, the most auspicious of animals (real and mythical) are represented in abstract forms. Particularly distinctive is the design known as *taotie*, a highly stylized representation of a monster-like animal with facial characteristics split into two symmetrical halves, featuring exaggerated eyes, geometric horns, jaw with fangs, and other artistic stylizations. The *taotie* motif is found on bronze artefacts in particular, such as bronze bells (*nao*), but also on bone and clay flutes (*xun*) (Fig. 1.1). Another motif, found on stone chimes (*qing*), is of a stylized profile of the tiger, historically the most feared of all Asian animals and the focus of much ritual attention (Plate 2).

Were it not for the ancient oracle bone inscriptions (fourteenth to twelfth centuries BC), we would know almost nothing of these ritual instruments. It is clear that the Shang kings believed in a powerful spirit world, whose force could be predicted by specially trained diviners. As the basis for prediction, shoulder bones of cattle (or tortoise shells) were inscribed with messages. The bones were then heated,

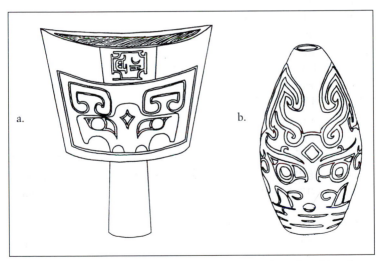

**1.1** Shang instruments with *taotie* motif: a. *Nao*—short, broad hand-held bell without clapper (height: *c.*15 cm); b. *Xun*—globular flute with three fingerholes in front, two thumbholes at back (height: 5.3 cm). Line drawings based on *c.*12th-century BC artefacts.

causing cracks to appear, and the cracks were interpreted. These artefacts were subsequently discarded or buried, where they remained unnoticed for more than three thousand years, until early twentieth-century scholars observed local farmers grinding them up for fertilizer. More than 100,000 pieces have been recovered and the fascinating field of 'oracle bone' research developed.

Most of the early characters in these inscriptions are pictographs, visual representations of material culture. Close to a dozen graphs picturing musical instruments have been identified and equated with modern characters. Some of these pictographic principles can be seen in the ancient graphs for drum, stone chime, and panpipe (Fig. 1.2). The Shang graph for *gu* drum (1.2a) shows a round drum on a stand, with an ornament on top; next to this (on the right) is a hand holding a stick in striking position. The present-day character is merely an abstraction of this pictograph. The graph for *qing* stone chime (1.2b) is similarly constructed, with a triangular stone suspended by cords (on the left), and next to it a hand holding a beater. The present-day character is a derivation, except that the radical for 'stone' has been added underneath.

| | Shang oracle bone graph | Han seal graph | Modern character |
|---|---|---|---|
| a. Drum (*gu*) | | | |
| b. Stone chime (*qing*) | | | |
| c. Panpipe (*yue*) | | | |

1.2 Pictographic characters for three Shang instruments.

Finally, the ancient *yue* panpipe (1.2c) is represented by two vertical pipes, with blowholes (or 'mouths') shown at the pipe tops, and a strip of rattan (or other) binding around the pipes. In its modern form, three pipes (and blowholes) are shown, together with a triangular hat-shaped element (possibly suggesting 'unification') and the radical for 'bamboo' added above the graph (clearly denoting its material of construction). Other graphs which have been definitively identified include the mouth organ (*he*) and the concepts for 'music' (*yue*) and 'dance' (*wu*). Future research is likely to clarify the ancient graphs for bells (e.g. *ling, yong*) as well. Owing to the very presence of their graphs in the bone inscriptions, these instruments were obviously of great ritual importance in addressing the spirit forces.[3]

## Zhou and Han Finds

Instruments uncovered from Zhou-period sites (11th to 3rd centuries BC) are of very great number and diversity. The most extraordinary of these sites is the fifth-century BC tomb of the Marquis Yi of the former Zeng state (Zenghouyi, Hubei province), which has yielded what seems to be a full ensemble of beautifully lacquered ancient ritual instruments, the most important being a visually stunning set of sixty-four externally struck bells (plus one additional large bell), suspended from an ornate three-tiered frame (*bianzhong*, Plate 3), and a complementary set of thirty-two five-sided stone chimes, suspended in a two-tiered frame (*bianqing*). Wind instruments include two transverse flutes (*chi*) with fingerholes on one side rather than on the top, two panpipes (*paixiao*), each with thirteen tubes of bamboo arranged in 'single-wing' form (Plate 4), and six mouth organs (*sheng*), with varying numbers of bamboo pipes inserted into gourd windchests. Zithers and drums are also represented, notably a ten-string zither (*qin*) with short soundboard, twelve large zithers (*se*), and a large barrel-shaped wooden drum (*jiangu*) mounted on a thick vertical post.[4]

In terms of instrument construction, acoustical sophistication, and decoration, the Zenghouyi ensemble is unquestionably the most important archaeological find in Chinese music history. As seen in Plate 3, this massive *bianzhong* bell set is comprised of three basic types: forty-five obliquely suspended bells with leaf-shaped cross sections, concave mouths, and shanks (handle-like extensions) on their crowns (*yongzhong* type); nineteen vertically suspended bells, similar to the above design but with suspension loops (*niuzhong* type, top tier); and one large vertically suspended bell, with elliptical cross section and flat mouth (*bozhong*, bottom tier at centre). The shank-type bells in particular have attracted close examination (Li 1996: 177 ff., Shen 1986: 53 ff.), not only for their massive size and beauty, but also because inscriptions on each bell indicate that not one but two pitches can be obtained, depending upon striking location—the primary pitch produced at the centre of the striking area, the secondary pitch (usually a minor or major third higher) near the left or right corner (Fig. 1.3a). The single flat-mouthed *bozhong*, on the other hand, sounds one pitch only. The set is fully chromatic throughout its middle range.

The various other Zenghouyi instruments are no less remarkable. The five-sided stone chimes (*qing*), for example, were cut according to specific dimensions. Indeed, the *Zhouli* text (Rites of Zhou [dynasty], *c.*3rd to 2nd century BC) lays out precise arithmetic proportions and angles for *qing* design (Fig. 1.3b): side A measured at one unit, side B at two, side C at three, side D at two-thirds of A, and side E a concave bottom edge. While the Zenghouyi chimes deviate in detail from this formula, the stone chimes in other ancient sets are very close if not identical.

Another example of advanced understanding in design and acoustics can be found in mouth organ (*sheng*) construction. On the ancient *sheng*, a variable number of bamboo pipes are mounted in a windchest of calabash gourd, the pierced neck of the gourd serving as a blowpipe. For each bamboo pipe, a free-beating reed of fixed pitch is attached (Fig. 1.3c).

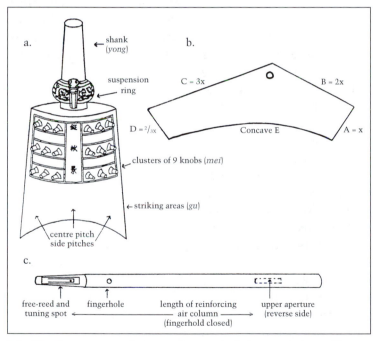

**1.3** Classic instrument designs and acoustical characteristics: a. *Zhong* bell with concave mouth, essential structural features; b. *Qing* five-sided stone chime, classical proportions (based on side A); c. *Sheng* mouth organ pipe, free-reed coupled with pipe.

The vibrating length of each pipe is necessarily tuned to the same pitch as the reed for the purpose of providing back pressure and resonance, without which the tongue of the reed could not vibrate. In order to prevent all pipes from sounding continuously, each pipe also has a small fingerhole which, when open, breaks the reinforcing air column, thereby preventing that reed and pipe from sounding. Covering a fingerhole allows a given pipe to reinforce its reed for vibration and, in this manner, several pipes can be sounded at once, enabling players to perform clusters of harmonically related pitches (as in contemporary practice). These and other complicated principles were already well established by the fifth century BC, though they were certainly based upon successful experiments of the Shang dynasty many centuries earlier.

Several interesting instruments have been found at other sites to the north of Hubei province, such as a thirteen-bell *bianzhong* and an unusual drum at the Changtaiguan tomb (Henan province). The bells are of the *niuzhong* type, with concave mouths and suspension loops. The number thirteen is of deep symbolic significance, found intermittently over the next thousand years in the numbers of panpipe tubes, sounding reeds in mouth organs, harmonic markers on the soundboards of *qin* zithers, frets on some lute-type instruments, and strings on *zheng* zithers and *konghou* harps. In medieval Chinese thought, the number thirteen represented the lunar cycle (twelve moons plus one intercalary moon) and it undoubtedly synchronized these instruments with cosmological belief. The drum type found at Changtaiguan, known today as a 'bird-frame drum' (*niaojiagu*), is suspended by cords between two carved wooden figures of large birds (most likely egrets) standing on the backs of crouching tigers. Many similar drums have been found in this historic Chu kingdom region of Central China, though specific design differs from one instrument to another (q.v. Fontein 1973: 66–9).

Perhaps the most surprising discovery from this period is of a *zheng* zither, found at a site in Jiangxi province. This zither, with sound chamber of wood and positions for thirteen strings, reportedly dates from the sixth century BC (an unusually early date, based entirely upon archaeological dating methods). The find is especially surprising because, while Zhou and Han sources had mentioned the existence of the *zheng*, it was clearly considered a 'popular' rather than ritual instrument, and (so the assumption went) should not have been appropriate for burial. Quite obviously, kings did not take counsel from musicologists.

Most significant among Han sites (206 BC–AD 220) containing musical instruments are Tombs No. 1 and No. 3 of Mawangdui, Hunan province, dating to the second century BC. Several instruments unearthed from these tombs are similar to the earlier finds, but others reflect differences in design: *se*, two twenty-five-string zithers, each with four top-mounted string-holding pegs and, remarkably, with silk strings and movable bridges intact (Plate 5); *qin*, one seven-string zither, somewhat similar in shape to the older Zenghouyi *qin* but with a longer soundboard and the now-standard seven strings; *yu*, two long mouth organs, one consisting of twenty-three pipes mounted in a wooden windchest, with many of its metal reeds intact. It is apparent from Han stone rubbings and other pictorial evidence that the *yu* and *se* were played together in ensemble, both within ritual and entertainment contexts (q.v. Liu 1988: 53–5, Mok 1978: 39–91).

# The 'Eight-Tone' Instruments and Confucian Ideals

Zhou court scholars can be credited with inventing the world's earliest system of musical instrument classification. While many instruments are mentioned in the *Shijing* (Classic of Songs, *c*.7th century BC), details are not available until later texts. The *Zhouli* identifies eight distinct resonating media or materials used in instrument construction—metal, stone, clay, skin, silk, wood, gourd, and bamboo—hence, the system name 'eight-tone' (*bayin*). In so classifying these ritual instruments, one of the primary motivations of scholars was to establish a system of cosmological correspondence with the eight trigrams (geomantic system of solid and broken lines), eight compass points, and other meaningful eight-part systems. It must be noted that bone, probably the most ancient of materials used in making flutes but no longer in vogue during the Zhou dynasty, failed to make the list.

Several characteristics of the ritual instruments are particularly noteworthy. First, the instruments embraced by the court—most having well-documented histories of over two thousand years—are believed to be indigenous and therefore specifically appropriate for ritual purposes. While several of these instruments have also become known among the general population, the majority have remained so closely associated with the Confucian ritual they have scarcely been seen outside the walls of the imperial palaces and shrines. Second, in both name and function, these instruments over time have acquired very close symbolic associations with the ideals ascribed to Confucius (*c*.5th century BC). Traditional Chinese government for most of the last two thousand years has attempted to use music to promote harmonious behaviour, notably by promotion of a 'refined music' (yayue)—to which the Confucian ceremony is believed to represent something of a preservation. Although the sombre Confucian rituals were mostly abandoned on the Chinese mainland, they have been maintained at several shrines in Taiwan, where many traditional practices can still be seen. Central to the music are the six hymns, simple and austere melodies sung in unison by a male chorus and (at the major shrines) accompanied by huge instrumental ensembles of nearly fifty musicians. All elements of the ritual—texts, costumes, dance, melodies, and instruments—serve to reinforce the Confucian ideology. For the 'eight-tone' instruments, the various metaphoric associations and iconic representations are so essential to their ritual functions, they will receive some emphasis in the following discussion.[5]

## Metal

Bronze casting, one of the great technological achievements of the Shang and Zhou dynasties, was employed primarily for construction of ritual implements such as vessels and bells. There is quite strong etymological and structural evidence to suggest that the Chinese clapperless bells nao and yong may have evolved from (or functioned simultaneously as) grain scoops. Other unmistakable associations between ritual instruments and agricultural practices will be cited below. Some bells, such as the elongated zheng (not the zither), were employed as signalling instruments on the battlefield, while others, such as the more standard zhong and bo, were used to punctuate ritual melodies in the large court orchestras.[6] Unlike Western bells, outer surfaces on Chinese zhong bells are typically decorated with raised rectangular ribs, repetitive claw-like, horn-like, or other zoomorphic designs and clusters of decorative 'nipples' around each bell, usually four clusters of nine each (Fig. 1.4a). When arranged in tuned sets, bells are referred to as *bianzhong* ('arranged *zhong*'). Unearthed sets from the Zhou and other early periods are of varying numbers (thirteen, fourteen, twenty-four, sixty-four, etc.), comprised of different-sized bells with concave mouths and leaf-shaped cross sections, suspended obliquely (if with shanks) or vertically (if with loops). From at least the twelfth century onward, the number, type, and arrangement of bell sets became more or less standardized at sixteen barrel-shaped bells of the same external size, suspended vertically by loops (Fig. 1.4b).[7]

Single bells, known as *bozhong,* are generally larger than *bianzhong*. Ancient *bozhong* usually have flat mouths and elliptical or round cross sections, their outer surfaces very elaborately decorated with abstract zoomorphic designs (including crouching tigers in high relief, Fig. 1.4c). On such bells, hanging loops are often in the shape of dragons or other auspicious animals. Largest among the bell types still in ritual usage is the *yongzhong* ('yong bell'), a single, oversized clapperless bell. *Yong* seems to be an onomatopoeic term (like *zhong*) of not very precise historical meaning, though generally referring to the largest of bells. Scholars believe that the *yong* bell was derived from the large Shang *nao* bell.

In the Confucian ritual, the various bells maintain different functions: *bianzhong* bells are used to play melodies (together with winds and strings); the medium-sized *bozhong* punctuates the hymn phrases; and the *yongzhong* is struck to signal the commencement of the ceremony.

## Stone

A natural substance from the earth, symbolic of longevity and stability, stone was of obvious value for usage in ancestral

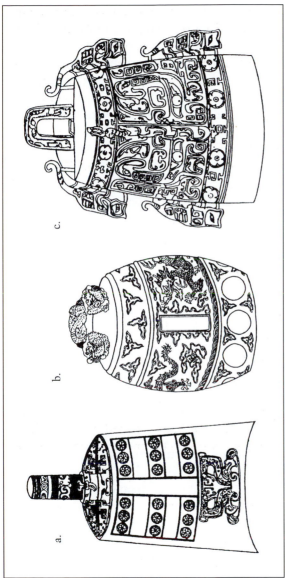

**1.4** Three clapperless bell types in eighteenth-century line drawings: a. Ancient-style *zhong* with shank (*yong*) on crown and side ring for oblique suspension, concave mouth; *bianzhong* sets are of different-sized bells (averaging between c.15 and 40 cm in height) (*Gujin Tushu Jicheng*, 1725); b. Qing dynasty-style *zhong* with loop (*niu*) on crown for vertical suspension, barrel-shaped profile with flat mouth; *bianzhong* sets are of the same size (height: c.24 cm) but of varying thickness (*Lülü Zhengyi*, 1713); c. Single *bozhong*, suspended vertically by a loop, with flat mouth (height generally between c.40 and 112 cm) (*Gujin Tushu Jicheng*, 1725).

rituals. Only one instrument type is found in this category, the *qing* stone chime. Single stones are known as *teqing* ('special *qing*'); sets of chromatically tuned stones are known as *bianqing* ('arranged *qing*'). Stones in the ancient sets are (like the bells) usually of similar thickness but of graded size. Instruments made between the twelfth and eighteenth centuries are more commonly of identical size but of graded thickness, and usually L-shaped in construction (unlike the ancient classical design shown in Fig. 1.3b). Sets of sixteen are most common for this period (Plate 6). In performance of Confucian ritual music, *qing* are employed to punctuate melodies in a manner similar to the bells.

## Clay

Clay is evocative of earth (*di*) as a fertile field. Constructed of fire-hardened clay, the *xun* globular flute is the only surviving example from this category. Following the appearance of the ancient Shang *xun* (Fig. 1.1), the globular flute is cited in the *Erya* (Refined Definitions, *c*.3rd century BC) as being of two types: large, shaped like a goose egg, with flattened bottom and six holes; and small, shaped like a chicken egg. 'Six holes' most likely refers to five fingerholes plus one blowhole (as on Shang types). By the eighteenth century, *xun* flutes commonly did have six fingerholes, four in front and two at the back (Fig. 1.5a), and subsequently eight or more fingerholes. Instruments surviving from this period are usually lacquered red and decorated with gold dragon motifs. While the iconic significance of the egg shape is not explained in the old texts, it is clear that the symbolic associations between the egg, earth, and fertility were quite ancient in China.

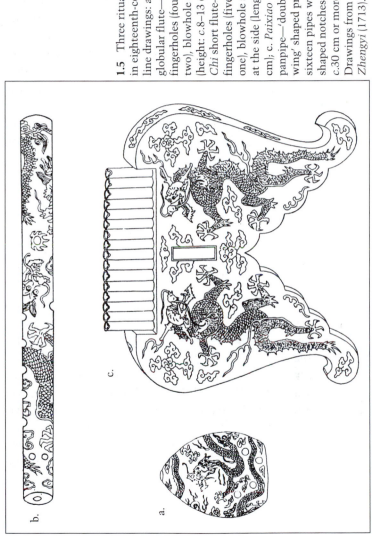

1.5 Three ritual flutes in eighteenth-century line drawings: a. *Xun* globular flute—six fingerholes (four plus two), blowhole at top (height: c.8–13 cm); b. *Chi* short flute—six fingerholes (five plus one), blowhole shown at the side (length: c.45 cm); c. *Paixiao* panpipe—'double-wing' shaped profile, sixteen pipes with U-shaped notches (width: c.30 cm or more). Drawings from *Lülü Zhengyi* (1713).

## Skin

Used for drumheads, the historic significance of skin is found in the signalling nature of the drums themselves (rather than, say, in communion with the hide-yielding water buffalo). More than twenty drum types are cited in the ancient texts, of which the *jingu*, *jiangu*, *taogu*, and *bofu* have survived in ritual practice. The *jingu* ('Jin [kingdom] drum'), like most ancient Chinese drums, has a barrel-shaped shell, onto which two drumheads are tacked. This drum, the largest in the Chinese instrumentarium, rests in a frame drumhead upward. According to the *Zhouli* text, the *jingu* was initially a military instrument, employed for issuing orders. A commentary on this text states that the diameter of the drumhead was '6.6 [Chinese] feet' (*c*.130 cm). While most drums of this type today are smaller, the magnificent *jingu* at the Beijing Confucian shrine is close in size to this ancient ideal (Plate 7).

More impressive in terms of decoration is the canopy-covered *jiangu* ('mounted drum'), a medium-large drum mounted on an anchored vertical post, drumheads sideward (Fig. 1.6a). Suspended over this drum is a richly ornamented canopy, with four colourful tassels hanging from its four corners (typically held in the mouths of carved dragons) and a carved egret on top of the frame. This canopy has been a consistent feature of the *jiangu* drum since it was first pictured in Han-dynasty art (q.v. Liu 1988: 30 ff.). A second drum of similar size but without the canopy, known as *yinggu* ('responding drum'), is also employed in ritual performances. Both are struck with unpadded beaters and utilized in percussion interludes between hymn phrases.

The *taogu* and *bofu* drums are smaller, but no less important. The *taogu* is a small drum (diameter: *c*.12 cm) mounted on a long round handle, with two short cords

**1.6** Ritual percussion in eighteenth-century line drawings: a. *Jiangu*— 'mounted drum' with canopy (drumhead diameter: between 60–80 cm); b. *Zhu* —box-shaped idiophone, decorated with images of mountains, clouds and water (*c*.60 cm square at top); c. *Yu*—tiger-shaped idiophone, with twenty-seven ridges on its back (length: *c*.60 cm or more). Drawings from *Lülü Zhengyi* (1713).

(attached to either side of the shell) with a bead on each end. When the handle is rotated, the beads alternately hit the heads in a rapid tremolo. Three short rolls signal the beginning of each hymn. The *bofu* (literally 'strike-slap') is a drum of moderate size (diameter: *c*.25 cm). It rests horizontally on a low rectangular frame and is struck with the hands to accentuate the beat of the hymns.

## Silk

Silk is the traditional material used in construction of strings. The *Liji* (Record of Rituals, *c*.1st century BC) suggests that silk strings represent 'purity' (*lian*) and 'determination' (*zhi*), an indication of the high value assigned by Confucian scholars to stringed instruments. During the ancient period, various zither types were differentiated, most significantly the scholar's *qin*, the ceremonial *se*, and the popular *zheng*. The *qin* is a small bridgeless seven-string zither, the paramount instrument of the Confucian scholar. The *se* is a larger zither, an exclusively ritual instrument, with twenty-five strings and movable bridges. These two zithers have been treated as a symbolic pair since their earliest documentation. The *Shijing*, for example, says of a happy marriage, 'good harmony between wife and husband is like playing the *se* and *qin*'. Indeed, this metaphor is current today, though usually stated in reference to a failed marriage: 'the *qin* and *se* are not in harmony'! Another related association with the Confucian value system is found in the *Liji*: 'the virtuous man [*zhunzi*], upon hearing the sound of the *qin* and *se*, thinks he is a very good person'. For the *qin* itself, which would become one of the most important of Chinese classical instruments, many other zoomorphic and cosmological associations emerged as well (further discussed in Chapter Two).

A very different perspective emerged for the *zheng*. Smaller than the large *se*, the *zheng* during its formative period existed in both twelve-string and thirteen-string varieties (this history sketched in Chapters Three and Four). That the *zheng* was a 'popular' instrument from the beginning is apparent from its omission from the ritual ensemble. Its etymology is revealing of the low social position this instrument was assigned, for its written character was derived from (and forever associated with) the ancient and inglorious ideogram for 'struggle' (rather than, say, with the positive values of 'harmony', 'reverence', or 'fertility'). As a consequence of this negative association, an invention myth emerged: in a 'struggle' between two people over a twenty-five-string *se*, the *se* was broken into two halves, resulting in the emergence of one *zheng* with twelve strings and another with thirteen. While this explanation is believed to be apocryphal, it is still very widely repeated today.

## Wood

Several highly idiosyncratic percussion instruments are included within this category, all with strong symbolic associations. The idiophone known as *zhu* is essentially a wooden box with outward sloping sides, open at the top (Fig. 1.6b). It is struck on the inside with a wooden hammer. Commentary in the *Shijing* notes that the *zhu* is like 'a lacquered grain container', suggesting a possible historic function within agricultural rites. Complementary to the *zhu* is another idiophone known as *yu*, a carved wooden image of a crouching tiger (Fig. 1.6c). In performance, a switch of wood or bamboo is drawn across raised ridges on its back, producing a rasping sound. The symbolic implications of this act are powerful, though never explicated in the ancient texts.

The tiger, lord of all Chinese animals, was once common throughout China and is associated with many qualities, such as courage, vigilance, and military prowess. Popular sayings of today still recognize the importance of subjugating tigers and remaining alert to danger. In Confucian ritual performance, the beginning of each hymn is anticipated by three strokes on the *zhu*, and concluded by three strokes on the back of the *yu*—as if to make this beast purr.[8]

## Gourd

Calabash gourd historically was employed in the construction of windchests for mouth organs, though this material in itself appears to have been weak in symbolic associations (other than agricultural). Several varieties of mouth organs are cited in the literature, notably the *sheng*, the larger *yu*, and smaller *he*.[9] The *sheng* mouth organ, with its double-wing shaped profile of bamboo pipes mounted in a windchest (q.v. Chapters Three and Four), is believed to be emblematic of the phoenix. The second-century dictionary *Shuowen Jiezi* states that the *sheng* 'looks like the body of a phoenix; [its music is] the sound of the New Year [when] all things grow [*sheng*]'. Within traditional belief, the Chinese phoenix was thought to be a bird of great beauty, associated with reason, prosperity, and the birth of offspring.

## Bamboo

The naturally hollow interior of bamboo is believed to be symbolic of humility and modesty, its hardiness in winter of human endurance and longevity. Over a dozen flute names appear in Zhou texts, though most of these are size variants for three basic types: transverse flutes, vertical flutes, and panpipes. The earliest transverse flute to appear in China was known as *chi* (Fig. 1.5b), an instrument constructed from a bamboo variety of relatively large internal diameter (*c*.3 cm). Unlike the arrangement on Western flutes and the later Chinese *dizi*, its six fingerholes were most commonly positioned on the side of the tube rather than in line with the blowhole (on top).[10] The *chi* is historically associated with the *xun* globular flute as a related pair. Their significance within Confucian ideology is noted in the ancient text of the *Shijing*: 'the elder brother plays *xun*, the younger brother plays *chi*', with further explanation in the text commentary that 'our minds, as brothers, must be in harmony', a metaphoric reminder of the need for familial accord.

Vertical flutes and panpipes were known by various names, depending upon the period. The flute today known as *xiao* is a vertical flute, with a notch at the blowing end (to facilitate tone production), five frontal fingerholes, and one thumbhole. It is clearly one of the most venerated of Chinese instruments, with an extended history in both ritual and common-practice music (q.v. Chapters Three and Four). Known by its ancient name *di*, the vertical flute was symbolically linked to the Confucian concept of *di*, a different character meaning 'to wash away evil from the mind'; i.e. through performance on the flute, one dispels malefic thoughts. For this instrument, quite striking continuity is found in today's practice, the *xiao* repertory tending to be dominated by the old and slow melodies of introspective character.

The Chinese panpipe, anciently known as *yue* (introduced above) and subsequently as *xiao*, was called *paixiao* (literally 'row *xiao*') by about the twelfth century, in attempt to distinguish it from the vertical flute. As discussed at the beginning of this chapter, the earliest instruments found were constructed of a series of thirteen notched bamboo pipes in the form of a 'single wing' (i.e. long pipes at one end). By the eighteenth century the prevailing shape had changed to a 'double wing' with sixteen pipes (Fig. 1.5c) (q.v. Chuang 1963). The panpipe is specifically associated with Confucian ideology by its historic name *xiao*, its character graph derived from the term *su*, 'respect'. Many texts also associate the panpipe with the legendary phoenix (*fenghuang*), both in terms of its sound and its wing-like profile. However, as seen in the decoration of all the eighteenth-century flutes illustrated in Fig. 1.5, instruments employed in rituals of the imperial palace were sometimes assigned to the realm of the legendary dragon (*long*). The image of a scaly, five-clawed dragon is a very common decorative feature on many ritual instruments. Unquestionably the most potent and multivalent of symbols within Chinese mythology, the legendary dragon was a beneficent spirit force, associated with heaven (*tian*), good fortune, male vigour, and indeed the emperor himself.

Of the very few ritual instruments accepted into common practice, the *qin* would become paramount among the literati class. It is introduced in the next chapter.

## Notes

1   Photographs and descriptions of these instruments can be found in a number of recent Chinese-language publications, notably those by Liu 1987, Liu 1988, Liu 1992, Zhao 1992, Li 1996, and in the many volumes of the anthology *Zhongguo Yinyue Wenwu Daxi* (1996–).

2   *Nao* bells have been found in sets of between three and five small hand-held bells, and also as very large single bells (weighing between 60 kg and 155 kg) sometimes known as *yong*.

3   Tong Kin-woon, in his exhaustive study *Shang Musical Instruments* (1983), examines these and many other early graphs, together with a good deal of contextual information.

4   Photographs of the Zenghouyi instruments can be found in many sources, the most recent and best being the Hubei volume of *Zhongguo*

*Yinyue Wenwu Daxi* (1996–), 187 ff. For an excellent English summary of recent research, see So 2000.

5   English-language information on the ritual instruments is uneven. Chuang Pen-li has published thorough scientific studies on the Chinese *paixiao* (1963), *chi* (1965), *qing* (1966), and *xun* (1972), the last three in the *Bulletin of the Institute of Ethnology, Academia Sinica* (Taiwan). Other single instrument studies include Shen Sin-yan's acoustical study of bells (1986) and Alan Thrasher's historical study of the *sheng* (1996). Brief entries on most instruments can be found in *The New Grove Dictionary of Musical Instruments* (Sadie 1984).

6   Other early Chinese bell types include *ling* small clapper bells, *duo* clapper bells, *nao* broad clapperless bells, *chun* large cylindrical bells, pellet bells, and chariot bells. These types, most of which survived the Han dynasty only in underground burial sites, are well documented in Li 1996. English-language surveys can be found in Kuttner 1990 and Von Falkenhausen 1993.

7   The older, obliquely suspended sets with concave mouths were tuned by varying the size of each bell, while maintaining uniform thickness. Vertically suspended bells with flat mouths were tuned by varying the thickness of the bell metal, while maintaining a uniform size—thicker bells producing a higher pitch than thinner bells.

8   The hymn itself is accompanied by another wooden instrument known as *paiban* (or *shouban*), a clapper of six hardwood slabs (though anciently of bamboo) held between the two hands and 'clapped' together on strong beats.

9   The *yu*, a large *sheng*, had two ranks of twenty-two or twenty-three long pipes; the *he* was reportedly a small *sheng* type with thirteen pipes and reeds. Both disappeared after the Han dynasty. The ancient Chinese mouth harp, historically known as *huang* (and by many later names), while usually constructed of bamboo, was often assigned to the 'gourd' category as well, perhaps because of the acoustical similarity between its tongue (essentially a plucked free-reed) and that of the *sheng*.

10  Several other variants of *chi* existed as well, one with the blowhole at the centre of the tube, another with a raised mouthpiece near one end. The popular transverse flute known as *dizi*, on which blowhole and fingerholes are in line, appeared after the Zhou period (its early history summarized in Chapter Three). Perhaps because of its believed introduction from non-Chinese areas of Central Asia, and subsequent use in military ensembles, the *dizi* has not been imbued with the deep symbolic associations of the other flutes. It has, nevertheless, been included in the ritual ensemble for many centuries, often ornamented with a carved dragon head and tail, and identified as 'dragon-head flute' (*longtou di*).

# 2

# Han Literati and the *Qin*

DURING THE IMPERIAL period, the affairs of government were handled by scholar-officials who had attained their positions, in large part, through their willingness to be educated into Confucian doctrine. Comprised of scholars, their families, wealthy individuals, and others with leisure time, this class of literati became the most ardent consumers of traditional high culture. For them, the *qin* zither was thought to represent the highest achievement in music. It was not, however, the only revered instrument. The *xiao* end-blown flute was also held in high esteem and performed solo or together with *qin*; and among the Hakka and Chaozhou (Chiu Chow) people of South China (where the *qin* is not generally played), the instrument most specifically associated with Confucian values is the *zheng* zither. Similarly, among the Minnan people of coastal Fujian province and Taiwan, the refined ensemble tradition known as *nanguan*, performed entirely on non-zither instrument types, is reflective of these same values (q.v. Chapters Three and Four).

## *Characteristics and Ancient Values*

The *qin* is a bridgeless, seven-string zither, approximately 120 cm in length. The term *qin* (pronounced as 'chin') refers both to the zither and more generally to stringed instruments as a categorical term. Consequently, the name *guqin* ('ancient *qin*') has become common as a means of distinguishing it from other stringed instruments such as *yangqin* (dulcimer) and *gangqin* (piano).

The body of the instrument is carved from two pieces of very old, dry wood: a top board with a gently arching surface (forming a fingerboard), and a flat baseboard with two soundholes.[1] After assembly, the shell is treated with several applications of a hard indigenous lacquer containing dyes, crushed deer horn, and other secret substances. An especially significant characteristic of this lacquer is the appearance on its surface of cracks (*duanwen*) as the instrument ages. Different patterns are recognized and actually given names (largely according to shape and age), such as 'plum blossom' cracks, 'cow hair' cracks, and 'snake belly' cracks. Rather than indicating need for repair, the presence of cracks is thought to add to the beauty of older instruments (similar to the effects of cracking on surfaces of fine ceramics).

The instrument's seven silk strings are of graded diameters, fastened at the plucking end to individual tuning pegs (by way of twisted cords), then wrapped around the opposite end and tied to two rigid string-holding 'feet' mounted in the baseboard. Vibrating length of the open strings (which are all of the same length) is defined by two fixed nuts, one at each end. Positioned along the length of the instrument are thirteen markers (*hui*), small circles of mother-of-pearl, jade, or other material inlaid on the fingerboard. Placed in exact correspondence with the overtone series, these markings serve to identify the positions of the harmonics (which are frequently employed in performance) and as general reference points for stopping of the strings.

The line drawing in Fig. 2.1 illustrates the shape and various parts of the instrument, front and back, together with some of its colourful nomenclature. Several names, such as 'phoenix eye' (a leaf-shaped pattern carved into the instrument head) and 'dragon pond' (large sound-hole through the bottom), derive from ancient cosmology and observations

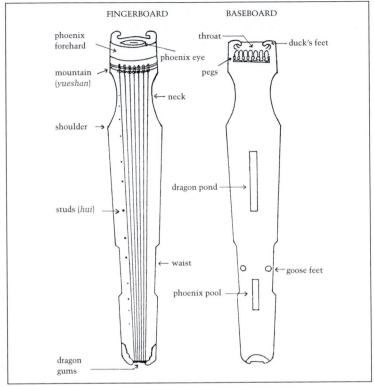

**2.1** *Qin* design and nomenclature; line drawing from *Meian Qinpu* (1931), with clarifications and additional nomenclature by Tong Kin-woon (1973: 122).

of the physical world. As seen in Chapter One, most of the 'eight-tone' instruments were assigned symbolic associations with auspicious animals, mythical and real, the dragon, phoenix, and tiger being especially prominent. The *qin*, however, venerable instrument of the sages, was considered to be of such great significance that it was assigned further symbolic associations. Its shape, for example, is explained in terms of anthropomorphic characteristics, as seen in names such as 'neck', 'shoulder', and 'waist'. Its length, at 3 feet plus 6.5 inches (in traditional Chinese units), is said to represent the number of days in one year (365) and its thirteen inlaid markers, the lunar cycle (i.e. twelve moons plus one intercalary moon). Thus, from a symbolic perspective, the instrument can be seen as a reconciliation of three basic elements of Confucian cosmology: the physical world (or earth), humankind, and heaven (*di, ren, tian*).

Confucian values were absorbed into *qin* mythology as well. The second-century AD book *Fengsu Tongyi* (Meaning of Popular Customs) states that '*qin* means *jin*', *jin* referring to 'restraint' from falsehood or bad deeds. By extension, performance on the *qin* is believed to have the power to calm emotions and promote virtuous behaviour.[2]

## History and Performance Milieu

Largely because of its elevated position within the scholarly tradition, the *qin* has been better documented than any other single instrument. Most likely derived from an earlier Shang-dynasty zither type[3], the *qin* was first mentioned in several poems in the *Shijing* (*c*.7th century BC). Context suggests that the instrument during this period was employed in both ritual ceremonies and for personal entertainment. Later references in the classic texts actually list the names of known scholar-performers, among whom the most famous was Confucius himself. Several ancient types of *qin* have been uncovered from archaeological sites, notably a fifth-century BC ten-string *qin* with short fingerboard, and a second-century BC *qin* with longer fingerboard and the now standard seven strings (q.v. Liu 1988: 22, 56–7, Liu 1992:

196–7, and So 2000: 65–85). The instrument attained standardized form soon after this.

Most significant for *qin* documentation are the dozens of treatises, essays, and handbooks, the earliest including Cai Yong's second-century AD treatise *Qin Cao* and Ji Kang's famous third-century essay *Qin Fu*. Ji Kang[4] was a *qin*-playing intellectual who argued that emotive states in music derive from listener interpretation, rather than from inborn (or 'universal') associations with the melodies themselves—an observation of great insight made seventeen hundred years in advance of similar postmodern thought in the Western world.

It is clear that the *qin* was well established among the literati by the time of the Tang dynasty (618–907), for it was mentioned frequently in the poetry and other literature of the period. Instruments and music (in descriptive notation) actually survive from this period. Shown in Plate 9 is one of these Tang treasures, an instrument with beautifully mottled red-brown lacquer cracked laterally in 'snake belly' patterns. Regional schools became established following the Tang, including the old and venerated Shupai (in Sichuan province), the equally famous Wupai (in southern Jiangsu province), and several others. Each had famous teachers, localized versions of repertory, and slightly different performance characteristics.

Since the *qin* was associated with the most ancient of values, scholars were inclined to possess one whether or not they knew how to play. Such instruments were usually hung on walls of private libraries. Robert van Gulik observed that '. . . the great majority of the literati, if they played [*qin*] at all, contented themselves with being able to play only two or three of the simpler tunes or even but a few bars' (1940: 19). Primary motivations for performance have traditionally included self-cultivation (mentioned in the Classics), identification with ancient heritage, and personal entertainment, rather than development and performance of a concert repertory.

*Qin* performance came under the influence of Daoist (Taoist) as well as Confucian philosophy. Some scholars retired to the mountains where, amongst the natural setting of pine trees or bamboo, and near flowing water, they would regulate their breathing, meditate, and play *qin*. Within this environment, performers could hope to achieve the Daoist quality of 'quiet' or 'inner stillness' (*jing*). Now the *qin*, with its strings of silk and small resonating chamber, is a naturally soft instrument; but some reclusive performers, we understand, sought to achieve absolute 'quiet' by actually de-stringing their instruments!

Painters over the last millennium have very frequently depicted reclusive *qin* players in their landscapes. Shown in Fig. 2.2 is one of the earliest visual representations of a *qin* performer, an anonymous line-painting on brick dating to

**2.2** Bearded *qin* performer, *c.*5th-century AD brick painting; line clarification by C. Fan, dotted lines suggesting original contour on defaced area.

29

about the fifth century AD. The instrument is shown balanced on the player's lap (reflective of the early performance position), the strings being plucked by fingers of the left hand and stopped by the right thumb (opposite from today's practice).

By the twentieth century, performance occurred most commonly in the home, where men and women of letters met to socialize, exchange ideas, drink tea, perhaps eat a meal together, and participate in the traditional arts. This type of meeting of the literati, known as *yaji* ('refined gathering'), became a major institution for the preservation of upper-class traditions such as *qin*, *kunqu* (opera songs), calligraphy, painting, and oral literature. Shown in Plate 10 is the noted scholar-performer Wu Zhao playing *qin* at a 1999 *yaji* in Beijing.

## Repertory and Style

Extending back over its long history, many hundreds of pieces have been notated in more than 150 *qin* handbooks, among which the early fifteenth-century *Shenqi Mipu* (with sixty-three pieces in tablature notation) and the popular early twentieth-century *Meian Qinpu* are particularly well known (q.v. Liang 1972: 46 ff.). The Hong Kong scholar-performer Tong Kin-woon has estimated that about 130 pieces are played today, though only twenty or thirty with regularity. A small sampling of the most famous pieces must include *Guanshan Yue* ('Moon over the Mountain Pass'), the very introspective *Yi Guren* ('Thinking of an Old Friend') and the cheerful *Meihua Sannong* ('Plum Blossoms, Three Variations'). There are many other well-known pieces in the repertory as well.[5]

*Qin* performance techniques are more numerous and varied than those of any other Chinese (or non-Chinese) stringed instrument. Open strings and harmonics are performed in a manner similar to the alternating out-in plucking techniques employed on Western lutes. Stopped strings, however, require a very wide variety of left-hand techniques, including ascending and descending portamenti, left-thumb pluck, numerous types of vibrato, and the wonderfully suggestive directions 'move like a crab' and 'drop like a waterfall'. This information is all contained in a complex tablature notation, with four or five directions given for each note (q.v. Lui 1968: 179–204).

*Yuluo Chunxiao* ('Spring Awakening at the Jade Pavilion') will serve as a brief example of *qin* style (the beginning shown in Fig. 2.3). The title suggests the early dawn on a spring day, the first rays of sun striking a mountain pavilion. The piece begins and ends, like many other *qin* pieces, with short sections entirely in harmonics. Harmonics, known as

**2.3** *Yuluo Chunxiao*, partial transcription. Transcription signs for selected idiomatic techniques: harmonics ( ᵒ ); short sliding approach to a pitch, up or down ( ↗ ↘ ); extended portamento on same string ( ); note bend on same string ( ); articulations deriving from a left-finger striking or plucking a string ( ). Source: *Meian Qinpu*, 1931 (of earlier repertory), transcription of 1974 performance by Tong Kin-woon.

'heavenly sounds' (*tiansheng*), are considered the most noble of all tones. The section that follows (Section 2) is performed on stopped strings, and requires extensive left-hand movement, notably portamenti or slides (shown with arrows), thumb articulations, note bends, and other techniques.

## Aesthetics

The Han literati, and those who aspired to their esteemed position, drew heavily upon Confucian values for the basis of their aesthetic system, though these values were often blended with the more creative ideals of Daoism. To apply a phrase of Joseph Levenson, the primary artistic aspiration of the literati can be described as the 'amateur ideal'—'amateur' here referring to the educated person with proper ethical training who participates in the fine arts during leisure time for self-cultivation. Within this context, 'amateur ideal' does not imply lack of training or low quality of performance, for the Han literati were often highly skilled in the arts. While there certainly was specialization in the traditional arts, professionalism (i.e. acceptance of financial return) was regularly criticized, in part due to its association with the attitudes of merchants, entertainers, and the ethically untutored.

Important aesthetic characteristics of the Han literati are reflected in both performance attitudes and in the music itself. The old text *Yueji* (Record of Music, a section within the Confucian classic *Liji*), in discussion of ritual and musical ideals, suggests that 'too many (ritual) forms will result in "chaos", too much (musical) invention will result in "violence"'. Traditional emphasis upon the old ways, expressed here in unusually rich hyperbole, has indeed cast a long conservative shadow over Chinese creativity. In fact, there has indeed been musical change and innovation over the past several thousand years, but the Chinese literati have usually opposed change in principle and made an institution of reverence for the old. In painting and music, the term *guya* ('ancient and refined') is regularly used in identification of those works reflecting a high degree of continuity with the past. This continuity is especially strong in the *qin* tradition, where the venerable old melodies are considered the best and the instrument itself has changed the least.

In keeping with the behavioural expectations of Confucian 'moderation', traditionally trained musicians also value restraint in all aspects of performance. The term *hanxu* ('covered and controlled') is used in reference to the deep and profound meanings which are concealed under an ordinary surface, or to an internal richness 'covered' by external plainness. In traditional landscape painting, there is a preference for monochrome and muted colours (over bright colours), often merely the suggestion of a subject, and the subtle concealment of good brush technique. In traditional *qin* performance, the player keeps his body and head still, showing no emotion, with eyes fixed on left-hand movement only. The emotive qualities of melodies are usually underplayed, embellishment minimized, and the demonstration of technical dexterity carefully 'controlled'. Indeed, when musicians refer to the admirable qualities of others, they say he/she has good 'style' (*fengge*), rather than good 'technique' (*jichao*). Disdain for virtuosity runs like a thread through the patterns of behaviour and artistic belief of the Han literati.

Chinese aesthetic ideals have also been heavily influenced by the philosophies of Daoism. The Daoist ideal of *ziran* ('natural' or 'intuitively from the self') refers to the rejection of artificial forms and processes. According to Daoist thought, the most interesting creative results are achieved through the application of 'natural' means, by intuition rather than by methodical planning. In art, the Daoist classic *Zhuangzi* (*c*.3rd century BC) states that line and form should not be strictly controlled, but 'curved without the help of arcs, straight without [artificial] lines'. In music, a similar philosophy is manifest in the presence of irregular phrase lengths, irregular repetitions, and, in performance, spontaneous improvisation and reliance upon memory (with its 'natural' lapses). These characteristics are especially prevalent in *qin* repertory (as seen in Fig. 2.3), in part because this is a predominantly solo tradition.

As a final observation, virtually all Chinese music is associated with cultural imagery. To be meaningful to composers, performers, and listeners alike, *qin* music must be based upon (or at least named after) the old legends, historic events, elements of nature, emotive states, or qualities of mythic animals. In the *qin* tradition (and in the visual and literary arts as well), this relational quality is called *yijing* ('spirit'). The 'spirit' or meaning of each piece is suggested by its title and affectively embodied in melody and in texts (if present) as well. For example, in the well-known *qin* piece 'Plum Blossoms, Three Variations' (*Meihua Sannong*), a short rondo-like theme performed entirely in harmonics is suggestive of the beauty and delicacy of the blossoms; this theme is followed by longer animated sections (requiring strong left-hand portamenti), which to some performers suggest the wind blowing the blossoms, but not dislodging them. Imagery in the title, of course, serves as a general guide only; the process of interpretation is personal. At any rate, no traditionally trained performer would fail to observe *yijing* and perform accordingly.

The above ideals, taken together, represent a special strength and beauty in *qin* music. Some are also found in the conservative 'silk-bamboo' traditions, the subject of Chapter Four. But first, it is necessary to introduce the other common-practice instruments within their respective historical contexts.

## Notes

1   The fingerboard is usually constructed of a softwood known as *wutong* (*Firmiana platanifolia*); the baseboard is usually of *zi* wood (*Catalpa ovata*).

2   For a more thorough examination of *qin* ethos, see van Gulik's *The Lore of the Chinese Lute* (1940) and the *qin* chapters in DeWoskin's broader study (1982: 101 ff.).

3   The ancient character *yue* (now meaning 'music') is composed of two elements: silk strings and wood. Scholars theorize that this suggests the existence of zither-type instruments by about the twelfth century BC or earlier. For further discussion, see Tong 1984, XV-2: 68 ff.

4   The romanization for Ji Kang in Western scholarship is usually Xi Kang or Hsi K'ang.

5   Many *qin* notations are reproduced in Tong Kin-woon's *Ch'in-Fu* (1973), where the older *Qinqu Jicheng* (1963–) and other miscellaneous articles are reproduced.

# 3

# Common-Practice Instruments in Historic Perspective

WITH THE EXCEPTION of just a few ancient Chinese instruments, the instruments employed in traditional ensembles of today have been imported into China from elsewhere. Instruments such as the *dizi* flute, *guanzi* reed pipe, *huqin* fiddle, and *pipa* lute were introduced over the last two thousand years and subsequently accepted by the people. To differentiate these from the ritual instruments of the imperial court, they can be called 'common-practice instruments'. This chapter will focus upon the most significant of the common-practice instruments as they have emerged over time. Many will be discussed further within their performance contexts and illustrated in Chapters Four and Five.

## *Ancient Instruments in Common Practice*

Of the numerous instruments believed to be indigenous to China, only the *xiao, sheng,* and *zheng* have won popular acceptance. These instruments emerged during the Zhou dynasty (*c.*11th to 3rd centuries BC).

The *xiao* (pronounced as 'hsiao') vertical notched flute, with its natural 'bamboo' tone colour and association with ancient cultural ideals, is considered the most noble of Chinese wind instruments. The vertical flute was mentioned in the *Zhouli* (third century BC) by the name *di*. Several centuries later, the Han poem *Changdi Fu* ('long *di* poem') reports that the instrument had five fingerholes, four in front and one thumbhole at the back. By the eighth century AD, a variant known as *chiba* (literally '1.8 feet') had emerged. No flutes of this sort have been found in China, but based upon similar eighth-century (Chinese) flutes preserved in Japan, it is apparent that this instrument had six fingerholes, five in front and one at the back.[1] By the twelfth century, the vertical flute had become longer (*c*.60 cm or more) and was more commonly called *xiao* (Fig. 3.4). On the southeast coast of China, however, the name *chiba* was preserved (together with the term *dongxiao*, 'open *xiao*') in identification of their more moderate-length variant. Today, *xiao* types are found in most regional chamber music traditions (Plate 18).

The *sheng* mouth organ, with a nearly unbroken history of more than three thousand years, is among the oldest of Chinese instruments in contemporary usage. The *sheng* most likely emerged as a Chinese adaptation of the very ancient *hulu sheng*, the 'gourd sheng' used by tribal peoples of Southwest China. Several different mouth-organ types were recorded in the early literature (q.v. Thrasher 1996: 1–20). By the eighth century AD, the *sheng* had achieved its present-day form of seventeen bamboo pipes circularly inserted into a windchest of gourd or wood, with a free-beating reed of copper alloy mounted near the bottom of each pipe. Mouth organs during (and well after) this period commonly had long curving blowpipes allowing the instruments to be held at a lower position, presumably so that court officials could see the attractive faces of female musicians (Figs. 3.4 and 5.1). Today, the *sheng* with short blowpipe is regularly employed in the music traditions of Central-eastern and North China (Plates 21 and 22).

The *zheng* zither (pronounced as 'jeng'), a popular rather than ritual instrument (q.v. Chapter One), is a multi-stringed zither, with a pitch-defining bridge under each of its strings. The ancient performance position, shown in a fourth to fifth

**3.1** Pre-Tang chamber ensemble, consisting of (right to left) *zheng*, *pipa*, *xiao*, and *yaogu*; fourth to fifth-century tomb painting (Gansu province); line clarification by C. Fan.

century painting (Fig. 3.1), is similar to many other early representations. The instrument head is cradled in the lap of the performer (seated on the floor), with the far end sloping away and also resting on the floor (similar to the performance position of the Korean *kayagum*). By the eighth century, the *zheng* commonly had twelve or thirteen strings of silk (Fig. 3.5c), increasing to sixteen (ultimately of copper or steel wire) and, from the mid-twentieth century, to eighteen or twenty-one (q.v. Cao 1983: 1–16). In South China and sinicized areas of Vietnam, traditional performers still use sixteen-string instruments (Plate 20). Occupying an elevated position similar to that of the scholar's seven-string *qin* zither of North and Central China, the *zheng* in South China is specifically associated with the esteemed values of Confucianism, most particularly among the Chaozhou and Hakka subcultures.

## Silk Road Instruments and Ensembles

During the Han period (206 BC–AD 220), Buddhist ideas and material culture were introduced into China by way of the

**1.** Bone flute (*c.*22 cm), *c.*6000 BC (Jiahu, Henan province); permission of the Research Institute, Beijing.

**2.** *Qing* stone-chime with tiger motif (length: *c.*84 cm), *c.*12th century BC or earlier (Anyang, Henan province); permission of the Music Research Institute.

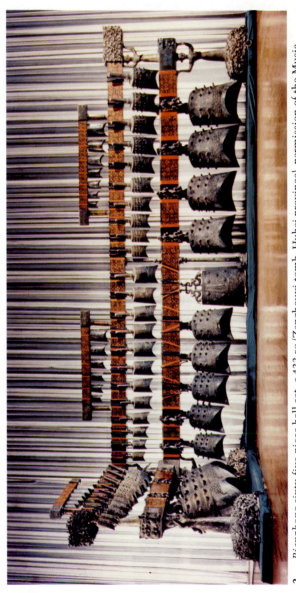

**3.** *Bianzhong* sixty-five-piece bell set, c.433 BC (Zenghouyi tomb, Hubei province); permission of the Music Research Institute.

4.   *Paixiao* thirteen-pipe panpipe, *c.*433 BC (Zenghouyi tomb, Hubei province); permission of the Music Research Institute.

5.   *Se* twenty-five-string zither (length: *c.*116 cm), second century BC (Mawangdui tomb No. 1, Hunan province); permission of the Music Research Institute.

6. Taipei Confucian shrine, with *bianqing* and other percussion on the temple platform.

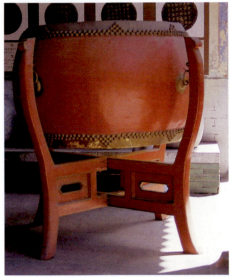

**7.** *Jingu* large drum
(diameter: *c.*130 cm),
Confucian shrine, Beijing.

**8.** Celestial musician with
*konghou* harp, Cave 285,
Dunhuang, third to fourth
centuries AD; permission of the
Music Research Institute.

**9.** Tang-dynasty *qin*, permission of the Music Research Institute, Beijing.

**10.** Wu Zhao performing *qin*, Beijing, 1999.

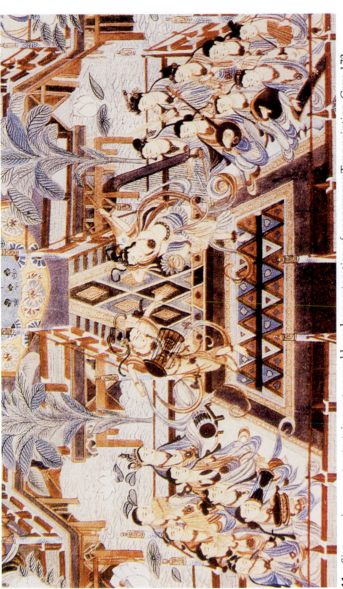

11. Sixteen-piece court entertainment ensemble, colour restoration of anonymous Tang painting, Cave 172, Dunhuang; permission of the Music Research Institute.

**12.** Celestial musician with *pipa*, Kaiyuan Temple, Quanzhou, ninth to fourteenth centuries.

**13.** Minnan musician Shih Lu with *pipa*, Lung-shan Temple, Lukang, Taiwan, 1984.

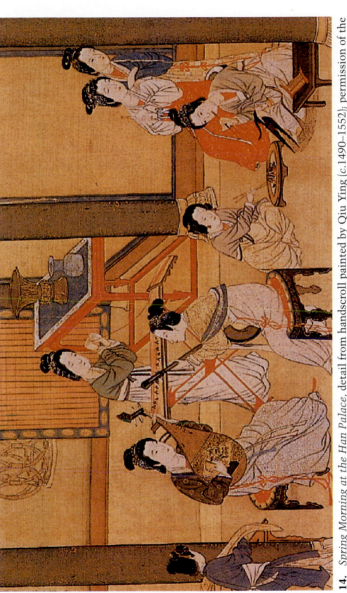

**14.** *Spring Morning at the Han Palace*, detail from handscroll painted by Qiu Ying (c.1490–1552); permission of the National Palace Museum, Taipei.

**15.** *[The Emperor] Returning to the Palace*, detail from handscroll, anonymous court artist (sixteenth century); permission of the National Palace Museum, Taipei

16. Hsien-he ensemble performing *nanguan*, Taipei, 1998.

**17.** Jiangnan *sizhu* ensemble, Huxing Ting teahouse, Shanghai, 1986.

**18.** Small Hakka ensemble, Rao Ningxin (*zheng*) and Luo Dezai (*xiao*), Guangzhou, 1986.

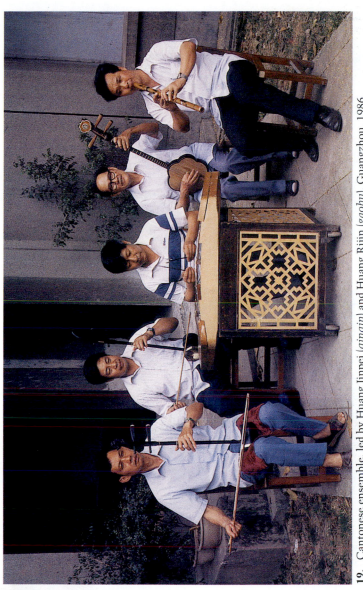

**19.** Cantonese ensemble, led by Huang Jinpei (*qinqin*) and Huang Rijin (*gaohu*), Guangzhou, 1986.

**20.** Han Mei performing traditional sixteen-string Chaozhou *zheng*, inlaid with mother-of-pearl designs, 2000.

**21.** Hou Shiquan performing *sizhu sheng*, Shanghai, 1990.

**22.** Shandong *guchui* ensemble, led by Liu Feng-sung (*suona*) and Liu Feng-tai (*sheng*), Taipei, 1978.

**23.** Guanghua Temple ensemble, *guanzi* and *sheng* in performance, Beijing, 1999.

**24.** Hebei *sheng-guan* ensemble in procession, with *yunluo* (front), *dizi*, *sheng*, *guanzi*, and percussion, Beixinzhuang, Hebei province, 1999.

so-called Silk Road, a long dusty caravan route connecting trading communities in Central Asia (and beyond) with North China. Imported instruments arrived in several waves. Among the first to be introduced were the *pipa* lute and *dizi* flute, two instruments which have become so thoroughly integrated into Chinese music they are now thought to be 'traditional'.

The *pipa* is well documented from the Han dynasty onward. Its name is reportedly derived from the sound of its playing action—*pi* (outward pluck) and *pa* (inward pluck)—though the possibility of this term being related to the similar sounding name of the ancient Indian *vina* is intriguing. *Pipa* was initially a generic term for different varieties of plucked lutes with fretted necks: the 'bent-neck' *pipa* with pear-shaped body and four strings (Fig. 3.4 and 3.5a); the straight-neck 'five-string' *pipa* (*wuxian*) with narrower pear-shaped body (Fig. 3.4); and even the straight-necked lute with round body and four strings (*ruanxian*) (q.v. Myers 1992, Zheng 1993: 21 ff.). On all types, elongated tuning pegs are inserted laterally into their peg boxes. Within a few centuries of its appearance, the bent-neck *pipa* (which came to dominate the other varieties) became fashionable in court entertainment ensembles. As shown in period reliefs and paintings, during the Tang period (618–907) the *pipa* was held in a horizontal position and plucked with a large hand-held plectrum, a performance position which was maintained well after the Tang (Fig. 3.4 and Plate 13). With the subsequent change to vertical playing position and use of fingers for plucking, the four-string *pipa* was embraced by musicians outside of court circles and it developed a very large repertory of solo pieces. The *pipa* today (Fig. 4.1 and Plate 17) is an indispensable instrument in most regional chamber ensembles.

One of these *pipa* varieties, the *ruanxian* or *ruan*, is believed by Chinese scholars to be indigenous, its name derived from that of the famous performer, Ruan Xian (third century AD). The *ruan* is distinguished from the pear-shaped *pipa* by its large fully round sound chamber and straight fretted neck. Although never quite as popular as the bent-neck *pipa*, within the recent few centuries it has spawned several generally smaller, better-known variants, notably the *yueqin* and *qinqin* (Fig. 4.1). The short-necked *yueqin* ('moon lute') is now used primarily in Beijing opera accompaniment. The long-necked *qinqin* ('Qin [kingdom] lute'), with its distinctively scalloped soundbox, is a member of both Cantonese and Chaozhou ensembles (Plate 19).

The *dizi* transverse flute, while not more important than the *pipa*, may be slightly better documented. According to Chinese sources, the *dizi* (or *di*) was introduced into China from Central Asia (Xiyu) early in the Han period. To what extent the ancient *chi* transverse flute influenced the development of the *dizi* is not clear. The *di* type, without the membrane hole characteristic of later flutes, was initially known as *hengchui* ('transverse blow') and used in outdoor military ensembles. During the Tang, the transverse flute was more commonly known by the name *hengdi* ('transverse flute'), though other names were used as well (Fig. 3.4). Employed in court entertainment ensembles together with *bili* (reed pipe) and *sheng*, flutes of this period had six or seven fingerholes, but still no membrane hole. The presence of an additional hole, to be covered by a thin vibrating membrane of bamboo skin, was first mentioned in the early twelfth-century treatise *Yueshu* (Treatise on Music), though not in specific reference to the transverse flute. During the sixteenth century, the flute with membrane known as *qudi* ('song flute', Fig. 5.1) became the lead instrument in accompaniment of *kunqu* classical opera, and it subsequently spread throughout the country. In North China, the short flute, *bangdi*, emerged about this same time.

Other more minor instruments were similarly introduced into China during the Han period, notably the *konghou* harp, an instrument type which existed in several variants. The most popular was the 'vertical' *konghou*, with curving upper frame and a lower string-holding arm at right angle to the frame (Plate 8). The *konghou* was listed in Tang records as an essential member of several different entertainment ensembles active at court, though its importance diminished after the tenth century and it eventually disappeared (q.v. Zheng 1993: 36 ff.). Long copper horns (*tongjiao*) and small reed pipes (*hujia*) were also introduced during the Han, their usage probably restricted to military functions and processions.

What type of music might these and the earlier instruments have performed? As shown by Han Kuo-huang (1979: 2), three broad ensemble types have been discernible

**3.2** *Guchui* military band with long horns and drums, fourth to fifth-century brick relief (Henan province); line clarification by C. Fan.

in China from the late Han dynasty onward—court sacrificial ensembles, processional ensembles associated with military or religious functions, and entertainment ensembles.

## Court Sacrificial Ensembles

Using the most ancient of Chinese instruments (sets of bells, stone chimes, etc.), ensembles of often massive size performed *yayue* ('elegant music') and other officially sanctioned music at established shrines in honour of heaven, the ancestors, and the sage Confucius (this tradition is briefly introduced in Chapter One).

## Processional Ensembles

Known by such names as *guchui* ('drumming-blowing') and, much later, *chuida* ('blowing-hitting'), processional ensembles performed for military functions and for auspicious events such as funerals (as they do today). Historically, such ensembles included long curved copper horns, transverse flutes of bamboo, and drums, instruments with loud, projecting volumes for outdoor performance. Shown in Fig. 3.2 is an early brick carving (*c*.4th to 5th century AD) depicting a small military band in uniform, two musicians playing long curved copper horns (*tongjiao*), two others playing medium-sized drums (*gu*) suspended at their waists. That other wind instruments were also employed in processional bands (e.g. panpipes and rudimentary reed pipes) is clearly shown on another brick found at the same site. Subsequently, reed pipes, shawms, mouth organs, gongs, and cymbals became more dominant in this type of music (Plate 24).

## Entertainment Ensembles

Utilizing a mixture of indigenous and imported instruments, entertainment ensembles performed a softer type of chamber music, to be enjoyed within the walls of the palace by attentive audiences. Two related genres of Han (and post-Han) entertainment music were regularly cited in early Chinese sources, *xianghe ge* ('harmonious song') and *qingshang yue* ('pure music'). While our knowledge of these genres is extremely limited and no music from this period survives, their general nature at least has been recorded, together with occasional references to instrumentation. As documented by Yang Yinliu (1981: 114), *xianghe ge* was a type of 'art song' in vogue among scholar-officials and merchants of North China, accompanied by 'string and wind instruments', the singer maintaining beats with a long stick (*jie*). A very early representation of a possibly related fourth to fifth-century chamber ensemble is sketched in Fig. 3.1, showing one costumed male musician playing *zheng*, together with three costumed female musicians playing *pipa*, end-blown *xiao* (or *changdi*), and *yaogu* hourglass drum. As will be seen, entertainment ensembles large and small have constituted a major category of music in China down to the present day (Plates 17 and 19).

## *The Eclectic Tang Ensembles*

Visual evidence concerning the make-up of entertainment ensembles between the fourth and tenth centuries is abundant. The Silk Road is lined with religious shrines built into cliffside caves. These shrines (still preserved more than 1,500 years later) contain larger-than-life statues and paintings of the Buddha, bodhisattvas, servants, dancers, and musicians. Earliest are the Dunhuang Caves of present-day northwestern Gansu province, begun in the mid-fourth century, with continuing artistic activity through the early tenth century. In fifth- and sixth-century wall murals, numerous very beautiful illustrations appear of 'celestial maidens' playing the prevailing instruments of the period.[2] Plate 8 shows one of these figures with a vertical *konghou* (harp), painted with highly imaginative curves and tasteful colours.

To the east of Dunhuang are the fifth-century Yungang Caves in present-day Shanxi province, and the early sixth-century Longmen and Gongxian Caves in present-day Henan province. A very good example of one of the many ensembles pictured in the Yungang Caves is shown in Fig. 3.3, a relief

**3.3** Pre-Tang Buddhist music ensemble, fifth-century stone relief in Cave 16 (left section), Yungang (Shanxi province). Left to right: *chi* (flute), *yaogu*, *pipa*, *tongbo* (cymbals) and, at lower left, *hailuo* (conch horn); reproduced by permission of the Music Research Institute, Beijing.

of five sensuous musicians in Indian dress performing (from left to right): *chi* flute (similar to the popular *di*), *yaogu* (hourglass-shaped drum), *pipa*, *tongbo* (small cymbals), and, at the lower left, *hailuo* (conch horn). Facing these musicians on a panel to the right (not shown) is the other half of the ensemble, five musicians playing *bili* (reed pipe), *konghou*, *paixiao* (panpipes), and two drums. Such ensembles of mixed winds, strings, and percussion appear to have been typical of the Buddhist-influenced music of the pre-Tang period. While there is some variation in instrumentation from one relief to another, for the most part ensembles are composed of two or three wind instruments (usually including *paixiao*, *di*, *bili*, and the conch horn), one or two plucked strings (usually including *pipa*), and one or two percussion (usually including an hourglass drum).

Most significant of the newly introduced instruments appearing in these pre-Tang paintings and reliefs are reed pipes, cymbals, and other percussion. The *bili* reed pipe emerged during this period, possibly as a lead instrument within the Kucha ensemble tradition (below). The *bili* is a short reed pipe of bamboo or wood, with large double reed and as many as nine fingerholes. It was assigned a central position in Sui and Tang court entertainment ensembles, a position preserved in the *hichiriki* role of Japanese *gagaku* music. Subsequently accepted into ensembles of North China, the *bili* is now known by the name *guanzi* or *guan* (Fig. 5.1 and Plate 23).

Small cymbals were introduced from India or Central Asia, mostly likely during the third or fourth centuries.[3] By the Tang period (618–907), cymbals known as *tongbo* ('copper cymbals') were named on instrumentation lists for the prestigious court ensembles. If the artwork of the period is reliable, these instruments measured about 20 cm or less in diameter (Fig. 5.2). Small gongs (*luo*) were also in use by the Tang dynasty, very possibly having been introduced from non-Han areas of South-central China. The standard instrument used in maintaining beats within the Tang (and later) ensembles was the *paiban*, a clapper constructed of five or six strips of resonant hardwood, bound together with a connecting cord through their top ends. While the Tang-style multi-strip *paiban* is still employed in Minnan music of southeastern China, the smaller three-strip *paiban* of North China appears to have been a more recent adaptation (Fig. 4.3).[4]

Drums (*gu*) were particularly numerous during the Tang period, the most important being *jiegu* ('Jie', a tribal name), a small cylinder or barrel drum with laced heads, resting on a low stand, reportedly used as a lead instrument in some ensembles; and the ubiquitous *yaogu* ('waist drum') or *xiyaogu* ('narrow waist drum'), a rather large hourglass drum with laced heads, similar in shape to an Indian *damaru* (though considerably larger), suspended from the neck of the performer by a strap (Figs. 3.1, 3.3, and 3.4). Other drums were documented as well, such as smaller hourglass-shaped drums resembling the *yaogu* (*maoyuangu, dutangu*) and a wide but shallow drum with laced heads (*dalagu*) (q.v. Zheng 1993: 42 ff.). These drums have clear affinities with Indian instruments. While they were very popular before and during the Tang dynasty, and most were passed on to Korea and Japan during this period of cultural contact[5], their importance in Chinese ensembles diminished greatly when China closed its doors to foreign influence after the tenth century.

During the Sui and Tang dynasties, entertainment ensembles received official patronage at court. Indeed, the emperors of this period became so enamoured with Buddhist exotica, they appointed many hundreds of musicians and dancers. As many as ten resident ensembles, the so-called *Shibuji* (literally, 'ten sections of skill'), were formed during the Tang—a massive undertaking in multiculturalism. Included were ensembles from India, Korea, Samarkand, Kashgar, and other areas of Central Asia, together with indigenous Han Chinese ensembles.[6] Instrumentation varied from one ensemble to another. Of the non-Han ensembles, the one from Kucha (formerly Guizi, present-day Kuqa in Xinjiang province) was particularly important. Kucha, like Samarkand, was one of the principal cultural centres of Central Asia during this period. If the instrumentation lists in the Tang source *Tongdian* (Encyclopedic History of Institutions) are to be believed, it is apparent that the Kucha ensemble by about AD 800 had already absorbed considerable influence from India, notably in the presence of conch horns, harps, and especially its many drums. The *Tongdian* list (which follows) is revealing. Winds: (*pai*)*xiao, sheng,* (*heng*) *di, bili, bei* (or *hailuo*). Strings: *pipa, wuxian* (*pipa*), vertical *konghou*. Percussion: *yaogu, jiegu, jilougu, dalagu, dutangu, maoyuangu,* and *tongbo.*

The Buddhist cave paintings at Dunhuang during this same period (*c.*9th to 10th centuries) depict many large ensembles with similar instruments, and show a blending of Indian/Central Asian and Han Chinese influences. One such ensemble is shown in Plate 11. This elegant sixteen-member ensemble is divided into two equal sections, positioned on either side of a central dance platform, upon which two dancers perform. Each carries a musical instrument, the dancer on the left a large *yaogu* (hourglass drum), the dancer on the right a *pipa* held behind the head. The instrumental division on the right consists entirely of the standard strings and winds (with the exception of the clapper); the division on the left, entirely of winds and

Indian-style drums (similar to those listed for the Kucha ensemble).[7]    Based upon the size and diversity of this ensemble, the animated dancers and sumptuous costumes, we can get an idea of the spectacular entertainment available to the Tang emperors and their guests.

The specifically Chinese ensembles in the *Shibuji* were of two types, *qingshang* and *yanyue*. *Qingshang yue* ('pure music') appears to have been a genre of refined court music, utilizing mostly ritual instruments (e.g. *chi* flute, *se* zither, *bianzhong*, and others). *Yanyue* ('banquet music') was a genre of entertainment music. It drew upon the talents of skilled musicians and dancers from outside the court who performed for banquets and other social occasions. Instruments employed in *yanyue* were similar to those in the Kucha ensemble, though usually including a set of tuned iron bars (*fangxiang*) and omitting the Indian-style drums, *konghou* harp, and conch horn. With only a few differences, this instrumentation is similar to that of Japanese *gagaku*, which was modelled after the Tang Chinese ensembles (q.v. Kishibe 1960–1, Picken 1969).

## Song Ensembles and the Huqin

Beginning with the Song dynasty (960–1279), changes in Chinese taste associated with neo-Confucianism and a renewed nationalistic spirit forced some foreign instruments out of fashion. In paintings of the period, the *konghou* (harp) and *wuxian* (lute) appear less frequently, and most of the nearly half-dozen Indian-style drums essentially disappear (at least in Han China). The *hengdi, xiao, paixiao, bili, pipa*, and *yaogu*, however, are regularly pictured in Song (and later) ensembles, together with *zheng, sheng*, and *paiban*. One of

**3.4** Early eleventh-century female ensemble, reconstruction by C. Fan of faded painting by Wu Zongyuan (c.990–1050). Clockwise (from top): *paixiao* (panpipe), *sheng, xiao, dizi* (or *hengdi*), *yaogu*, 'bent-neck' *pipa* and 'five-string' *pipa*.

several excellent illustrations of this smaller ensemble, reflecting a slight shift in instrumentation, is reproduced in Fig. 3.4, a black and white line reconstruction of a faded eleventh-century painting by the artist Wu Zongyuan (c.990– 1050). The painting depicts a procession of elegantly dressed 'celestial maidens', seven of whom play popular instruments of the period (though without *zheng*, *bili*, or *paiban*). While the painting is a rather romanticized depiction of a late Tang (reportedly 'Kucha') ensemble, it does show some of the prevailing instruments of the eleventh century and the continuing fascination with female ensembles.

Of all the instruments imported into China during the late Tang–early Song period, the *huqin* became most widespread. The name *huqin* (literally 'barbarian fiddle') emerged because the instrument was formerly associated with northwestern tribal peoples whom the Han Chinese imperiously called 'barbarians' (Hu). Subsequently, *huqin* became a generic term, identifying the entire 'family' of Chinese bowed string instruments. The earliest documented *huqin* type is the tenth-century *xiqin* ('Xi [tribal] fiddle'), an instrument with two strings activated by friction using a thin strip of bamboo. The *xiqin* (Fig. 3.5b) is one of many instruments depicted in the early twelfth-century treatise *Yueshu*. From about the thirteenth century onward, bows with horsehair strings (instead of bamboo strips) were employed on fiddles known as *mawei huqin* ('horse-tail *huqin*') (q.v. Stock 1993). By the sixteenth century, a variant called *tiqin* ('hand-held *qin'*) became popular in accompaniment of *kunqu* and the various regional operas. The *tiqin* sound chamber was constructed from a halved coconut shell. Its two tuning pegs were inserted laterally into the pegbox, and the horsehair on the bow passed between the strings (as it does on twentieth-century instruments).

50

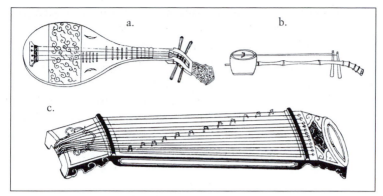

**3.5** Early 12th-century sketches of Tang–Song stringed instruments in the treatise *Yueshu*: a. 'bent-neck' *pipa*; b. *xiqin*; c. 'twelve-string' *zheng*.

Similarly constructed regional variants include the *banhu* of North China and the larger *yehu* of South China. The miniature *jinghu*, with tubular sound chamber of bamboo, was in use within the Beijing opera ensemble by the late eighteenth century. Today, *huqin* types appear everywhere in China, existing in dozens of regional styles and known by many names (Fig. 4.2 and Plates 16, 17, and 19; q.v. Moule 1908: 121–32). The *erhu* ('two [string] barbarian'), which emerged as recently as the early-twentieth century, has now become the most popular of these types, primarily as a concert-hall instrument.

Other instruments also came into prominence during and after the Song period, most notably the *sanxian* and *yunluo*. The *sanxian* (literally 'three string'), a long-necked fretless lute with small snakeskin-covered resonator (Fig. 4.1), was first mentioned in Chinese sources during the Mongol-dominated Yuan dynasty (early fourteenth century), though recent research has shown that similar instruments were known in China at least two hundred years earlier.[8] Most likely an adaptation of Central Asian three-stringed lutes (possibly *setar*), the *sanxian* is now widely employed throughout China in traditional opera ensembles, chamber ensembles, and in accompaniment of narrative song. The *yunluo* (literally 'cloud gongs') is a set of ten (or more) small basin-shaped gongs suspended in a portable frame (Fig. 5.1). Mentioned in the fourteenth-century history text *Yuanshi* and pictured in period art together with wind-and-percussion instruments, tuned gongs were employed in imperial processions from this period onward. Today, the *yunluo* is regularly used in rural processions and temple ensembles across North China (Plate 24).

The ready acceptance of these instruments by Chinese musicians is reflected in Song and Yuan visual arts and written documents. Among the most interesting of visual sources showing post-Tang instruments in ensemble is the medieval Kaiyuan Temple in the Minnan city of Quanzhou (southern Fujian province). The Kaiyuan is a Buddhist temple, initially constructed between the seventh and ninth centuries, subsequently destroyed and rebuilt in the late fourteenth century. Mounted under the eaves of one of the attached halls are twenty-four celestial musicians carved of wood, each holding a replica of a musical instrument. Instruments include *pipa* (held horizontally), *dongxiao* (southern style of *xiao* vertical flute), and *paiban* (clappers), all of which reflect construction details and performance positions similar to those of the Tang dynasty. A figure with *pipa* is shown in Plate 12. Also represented are the post-Tang instruments *erxian* (southern *huqin* type resembling the *xiqin*) and *sanxian*. Finally, the *sheng* and *yunluo* (both of which subsequently fell into disuse in South China) and a few other instruments are depicted as well (q.v. Zhao 1992: 54–61).

It is significant that the old and elegant Minnan ensemble of today (*nanyue* or *nanguan*) is based upon this core of Kaiyuan instruments: *pipa* and *dongxiao* (known locally as the 'host' instruments), *erxian* and *sanxian* (the 'guest' instruments), and *paiban* (Plate 16). The present-day Minnan instruments are also very close in design to those pictured in the hands of the Kaiyuan figurines (unlike the northern instrument variants which have undergone greater change). Some music scholars suggest, somewhat boldly, that Minnan music reflects Tang or pre-Tang practice—possibly even *qingshang* music. While the age of Minnan music is still a matter of debate, the composition of the ensemble as preserved may well have been in place by the fourteenth century, with roots extending back into the Song and Tang dynasties. Scholars of neighbouring Chaozhou and Hakka traditions make similar suggestions about their music, especially in reference to their historic solo *zheng* repertories.

## Late Imperial-Period Ensembles

By the Ming dynasty (1386–1644), basic instrumentations for chamber and processional ensembles had become well established, though experimentation within the imperial palace would continue well into the Qing dynasty (1644–1911).[9] It is clear from written documents, paintings, and continuous tradition that the core of most Ming–Qing chamber ensembles consisted primarily of bowed and plucked stringed instruments (*huqin*, *pipa*, *sanxian*, *zheng*, sometimes *ruan*), supplemented by winds (*di* or *xiao*, sometimes *guanzi* and *sheng*), and punctuated by light percussion (*paiban* in particular). Processional ensembles, on the other hand, consisted primarily of the louder wind instruments (*guanzi/bili* or *suona*, *sheng*, sometimes *dizi*), punctuated by tuned percussion (*yunluo*) and other heavy percussion (*bo*, *dangzi*, *gu*, etc.).

Music scenes from two Ming handscrolls will illustrate these different types. As seen in the early sixteenth-century handscroll, *Spring Morning at the Han Palace* (detail in Plate 14), the imperial fascination with 'silk-bamboo' (*sizhu*) entertainment performed by talented beauties continued well beyond the Tang. This handscroll reveals many leisurely activities within the palace grounds, notably of ladies attending to flowers, playing chess, reading, painting, and preparing for a musical performance. Shown in this detail is part of a small ensemble of female musicians, including (left to right): *pipa* (played with a plectrum), *zheng* (being restrung), *ruan* (in playing position), *sheng* (one pipe being tested), and *guanzi* or *bili* (held by the performer). To their left (an area not shown in this detail), two women dance; to their right (also not shown), other musicians approach carrying a flute (*dizi* or *xiao*), an instrument in a silk case (possibly a *huqin*), and a *qin* zither (which would not normally be played in ensembles of this size).

The second sixteenth-century handscroll, in contrast, shows male musicians performing outdoor 'blowing-hitting' (*chuida*) music (detail in Plate 15). This magnificent handscroll, entitled *Returning to the Palace*, depicts the journey of the emperor Shi Zong (r.1522–66) along a river, accompanied by barges of armed guards, ministers, and other functionaries, eunuchs with firecrackers, floating restaurants, and two full barges of musicians—nearly one thousand figures in all. On the two music barges, the costumed male musicians perform (left to right): *yaogu*, *paiban*, *xiao*, *guanzi*, *sheng*, *dizi*, *yunluo*, *bo* (cymbals), *gongluo* (knobbed gongs), *dagu* (large drum), and *dangzi* (small gong). The function of these loud ensembles (located on either side of the imperial barge) would most likely have been to surround the emperor with glorious stereophonic sound, and possibly to strike fear in the hearts of would-be assassins (if also having the effect of raising the imperial blood pressure).

Only one other instrument of enduring importance would be added to the *sizhu*-type ensembles, the *yangqin* (literally, 'foreign *qin*'), a trapezoidal-shaped hammer dulcimer traditionally with two rows of bridges and seven or more courses of metal strings running across each (Fig. 4.1 and Plate 17). The *yangqin* is an adaptation of the Persian *santur*, which was introduced into South China during the late Ming dynasty. Not included in the sixteenth-century ensembles discussed above, the *yangqin* became widely accepted in South and Central-eastern China during the centuries to follow. The most recent addition to *chuida*-type ensembles is the *suona*, a shawm-type double-reed instrument with flaring metal bell (Fig. 5.1 and Plate 22). Its name, *suona*, is a transliteration of the Arabic *zurna* or Central Asian *suernai*, instruments introduced to the Central Plain of North China by the Ming dynasty (though possibly known in far western China before this). Today, the *suona* is important in processions and traditional opera accompaniment.

Nearly half a dozen genres of surviving instrumental music are believed to have been in practice during the Ming–Qing period. *Shifan luogu* ('ten kinds of gongs and drums') is one such genre, a tradition of southern Jiangsu province employing (in one variant) both soft 'silk-bamboo' instruments (*di, xiao, erhu, banhu, pipa, sanxian,* etc.) and loud 'blowing-hitting' instruments (small *suona, sheng,* and a variety of gongs, cymbals, and drums). Another genre of percussion-dominated music in practice during the Ming (if not earlier) is Xi'an *guyue* ('Xi'an drum music'), centred in the city of Xi'an and other areas of southern Shaanxi province. Instruments include barrel-shaped drums, gongs, and cymbals, all in several sizes, together with the melody instruments *di* and *sheng* (and sometimes *guanzi*). Liu Dongsheng (1992: 291) and others suggest that, in terms of instrumentation and form, Xi'an *guyue* resembles the old *yanyue* ('banquet music') of the Tang court.

In Beijing and other urban areas of North China, a literati chamber tradition known as *xiansuo* ('string ensemble') is also believed to have been in practice by the Ming dynasty. A collection of thirteen *xiansuo* suites was transcribed during the early nineteenth century (*Xiansuo Beikao*, 1814), showing heterophonic details for four stringed instruments: *huqin*, *pipa*, *sanxian*, and *zheng* (to which wind instruments were added as needed). While the popularity of *xiansuo* chamber music had declined sharply by the mid-twentieth century, variants of many pieces are still known among older musicians. The *zheng* and *pipa* solo traditions also preserve well-established repertories from the Ming–Qing period.

The more cosmopolitan Jiangnan and Cantonese instrumental ensemble traditions (centred in Shanghai and Hong Kong respectively) are newcomers, both having emerged during the nineteenth and early twentieth centuries. While instrument usage and repertory are related to the earlier models, these ensembles tend to be dominated by the more recent *huqin* types (e.g. *erhu* and *gaohu*), together with flutes, plucked lutes, and *yangqin* (rather than *zheng*) (Plates 17 and 19).

Against this brief historical overview, we now turn to the social and performance roles these instruments play within the chamber ensembles of today.

## Notes

1   The Japanese pronunciation of *chiba* is 'shakuhachi', though the Japanese *shakuhachi* of today is a longer instrument, somewhat similar to the Minnan *dongxiao* but with fewer fingerholes. See Hayashi 1967 for examination of these and other eighth-century instruments.

2   A representative selection of photographs from various caves appears in volume nine of the series *Zhongguo Yinyue Shi Cankao Tupian* (1964). Considerably more comprehensive photo reproductions are found in the Gansu, Shanxi, and Henan volumes of the anthology *Zhongguo Yinyue Wenwu Daxi* (1996–). For Dunhuang alone, an excellent English-language source is Zheng 1993.

3   It is possible that some very small 'cymbals' were actually hemispheric bells (*ling*), which were of similar shape but had tuned pitches.

4   For a survey of the vast variety of idiophones in use during the late nineteenth century, including some used in narrative song accompaniment, see Moule 1908: 10–47. Good descriptions of reed pipes and horns are found here as well.

5   In Japan, the *jiegu*, known as *kakko*, is still in use; in Korea, the *yaogu* (or *zhanggu*), known as *changgo*, is also still in use; other historic drum types are preserved by tribal peoples of Southwest China.

6   The *shibuji* ensembles, as documented in the *Suishu* (Book of Sui [dynasty]) and the Tang dictionary *Tongdian*, are outlined in Cheung 1974: 127 ff and Yang 1981: 252 ff. For an English-language summary of this and other Sui–Tang music institutions, see Kishibe 1960–1: 14 ff.

7   The musicians are positioned in four rows (right to left): 1) *paiban*, *bili*, *xiao*, and *sheng*; 2) *zheng*, *pipa*, *ruanxian*, and *konghou*; 3) *dalagu*, *maoyuangu*, *jilougu* (with *taogu*), and *jiegu* (resting on a stand); 4) *hengdi* (flute), *hailuo* (conch), *paiban*, and *paixiao* (panpipe).

8   Other related lute types include the small pipa-shaped *hulei* (literally 'sudden thunder'), *liuyeqin* ('willow leaf' *qin*) and *huobusi* (literally 'fire-no-contemplation'). The snakeskin-covered *hulei* and *huobusi* were adaptations of Central Asian lutes, now obsolete in Han China. The *liuyeqin*, essentially a miniature *pipa*, is still in use.

9   In Han Kuo-huang's examination of the development of the modern Chinese orchestra (1979: 6), he outlines one of two ensembles brought into the imperial court from Mongolia during the seventeenth century. The basic instruments are those we would expect, but with several exotic additions: *tiqin* (in this case, a Mongolian four-string fiddle), *huobusi* (Central Asian *qobuz*), *erxian* (reportedly a lute in this ensemble), and *yazheng* (bowed zither).

# 4
## *Sizhu* Instruments

*Sizhu*, literally 'silk-bamboo', is a term used by Chinese scholars in collective reference to the chamber music traditions from Central-eastern China southward. *Sizhu* (pronounced as 'sih-ju') may be considered a type of 'chamber music' in the sense that it is a refined tradition, performed for attentive audiences in homes, music clubs, or teahouses. The name has arisen from the use of instruments with silk strings (lutes, fiddles, and zithers) and flutes of bamboo. Percussion instruments, when employed, are small in size and usually restricted to clappers, wood-blocks, and other time-markers. Chinese musicologists often contrast *sizhu* music with the more northern tradition of *chuida* ('blowing-hitting'), which is dominated by louder wind instruments together with cymbals, gongs, and drums. This relationship, however, is complex and will be taken up in Chapter Five.

The various Han subcultures maintain local names for their chamber traditions. The Minnan of southern Fujian province commonly refer to their music as *nanyue* ('southern music'), though their Minnan relatives in Taiwan use the term *nanguan* ('southern pipe'). Chaozhou and Hakka people of eastern Guangdong province refer to their music as *xianshi* ('string poem') and *sixian* ('silk string') respectively, though other names are used as well. In the Jiangnan area of Central-eastern China, the term *sizhu* itself is most common, but the Cantonese simply refer to their instrumental music as *yinyue* ('music'). Related ensemble types include the less widely known *bantouqu* of Henan province, *baisha xiyue* of western Yunnan province, and a few others.

## Social Background

As seen in Chapter Three, the concept of chamber music in China is ancient. Indeed, some instruments (such as *zheng*, *sheng*, and *xiao*) have changed but modestly since their early appearance. But there is little evidence to suggest that repertory resembling today's chamber music dates back any earlier than about the fourteenth century, which is approximately the time when the Indian-style drums and harps were falling out of fashion. By the sixteenth century, the 'silk-bamboo' ensembles associated with *xiansuo* chamber music and *kunqu* opera were clearly in place, and these traditions have lasted into the twentieth century.

*Sizhu* music, unlike the class-oriented *qin* tradition, is typically performed by musicians from diverse backgrounds and occupations—educated and uneducated, merchants and workers, well-dressed and plainly-dressed. Its social constituency is the entire culture of a region, not just one segment of it. The principle type of *sizhu* association is the music club. Since participation in instrumental ensembles requires leisure time (for development of skills and attendance at meetings), men dominate these clubs, perhaps because men in China have more spare time than women. Small cities such as Xiamen (Amoy) and Shantou (Swatow), located along the southeastern coast, have several music clubs each; the very large cities of Shanghai and Hong Kong have a dozen or many more. Music clubs generally meet once a week in large designated rooms. Meetings are very casual, musicians alternately performing in the ensemble, drinking tea, and talking with friends at the side.

In Chaozhou and Hakka cultures, where lineage is carefully preserved and large extended families live in close proximity, ensembles made up entirely of family members are common. Family ensembles are comprised of two or more generations of musicians with either direct blood ties or ties through relationship by marriage. Such ensembles tend to develop their own distinctive performance styles and forms, styles which often cannot be reconciled easily with those of other ensembles. Music clubs comprised of members not of one family also exist among these cultures.

Traditional performances occur at any of several venues. In the music clubs and family ensembles, musicians perform for themselves and for each other. This milieu is common in the performance of Chaozhou and Hakka music, though it is also found in varying degrees among all the regional traditions. For public performances, the teahouse and temple are the most common locations. The teahouse milieu is especially important in Shanghai. Without question the most picturesque traditional teahouse still in operation is the Huxing Ting ('lake-star pavilion'), a five-sided building standing in the middle of a large goldfish pond. People come here daily to drink tea and socialize. Every Monday afternoon musicians gather to perform Jiangnan *sizhu*. Comprised mostly of retired men and a few middle-aged men, the instrumentalists sit in a circle around one or two small tables (Plate 17). As in the club environment, musicians alternately perform with the ensemble and socialize with friends.

The temple environment is more common in performance of Minnan music, especially the tradition preserved in Taiwan. Facing the entrance of many Buddhist temples are outdoor stages for theatrical and musical performances. During religious holidays and on auspicious birthdays, performances of local opera and *nanyue* (*nanguan*) are presented before large audiences and in honour of ancestors and the Buddhist gods.

Performance of Cantonese instrumental music is unique among *sizhu* traditions. While Cantonese music was performed in teahouse settings during the early twentieth century, in the 1930s it was increasingly associated with the emerging technologies of film, radio, and the phonograph. When silent films were introduced into South China, for example, Cantonese instrumentalists played at intermissions—a short-lived association, but one that reflects upon Cantonese eclecticism. During this same period, Cantonese musicians took increasing interest in recording their performances and many 78 rpm recordings were made by the best musicians. As a result, the tradition became more unified than the other southern genres. A relatively new performance venue common in present-day Hong Kong and Cantonese communities of the Western world is the fund-raising concert. Typically held in large restaurants, such performances are dominated by concert versions of traditional opera songs, with some instrumental music performed during interludes.

## Instruments

Chinese chamber music is primarily string music. At the core of each ensemble are several or more stringed instruments, most notably the *pipa* lute, *huqin* fiddle, and *zheng* zither. Providing timbral contrast are softer wind instruments such as the *xiao* end-blown flute and, in some repertories, *dizi* transverse flute and *sheng* mouth organ. The emergence of these common-practice instruments has been outlined in Chapter Three. In the present chapter, they will be described more fully and discussed within their performance contexts.[1]

61

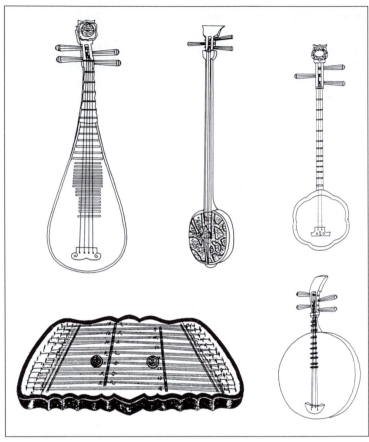

**4.1** *Sizhu* lutes and dulcimer. Clockwise (from upper left): *Pipa*, contemporary style, four strings (*c*.102 cm); *Sanxian*, three strings (*c*.97 cm); *Qinqin*, three tuning pegs but only two strings (*c*.92 cm); *Yueqin*, four strings (*c*.62 cm); *Hudie qin*, old-style *yangqin*, two rows of seven bridges (*c*.90 cm). Contemporary line drawings; *hudie qin* drawing from *Xiange Bidu* (1917).

## Lead Stringed Instruments

Most significant in the *sizhu* ensembles are the stringed instruments, lutes, fiddles, and zithers with strings of twisted silk (though now usually of metal). The lute *pipa* is used in all chamber traditions. The physical appearance of the *pipa* is striking. Its sound chamber is pear-shaped but quite shallow (relative to Western lutes). Four strings run between the string holder (glued to the soundboard) and four elongated, laterally inserted tuning pegs (Fig. 4.1). Frets lining the neck are of two types—triangular-shaped upper frets of hardwood, ivory or bone, and lower frets of bamboo strips extending down onto the soundboard. The characteristic (Jiangnan region) string tuning of A - d - e - a is unique to this lute (and, in performance, this tuning is occasionally used for harmonic effects as well). Plucked with plastic fingernails taped to the right-hand fingers, the *pipa* has become an instrument of the virtuoso, its solo repertory in particular requiring exceedingly agile finger action. In most areas of China, the lute now is held vertically, resting on the player's left thigh (Plate 17). Minnan musicians in coastal Southeast China, however, preserve the Tang-style *pipa* (with its wider sound-chamber and turned-back pegbox) and its horizontal playing position as well (Plates 13 and 16 and Figs. 3.1, 3.3, and 3.4).

*Huqin* two-stringed bowed fiddles are also widespread throughout China, though each region has its own variant. Chinese fiddles are constructed of a narrow pole of hardwood or bamboo inserted through a tubular or hemispheric resonating chamber. Two strings run from tuning pegs at the top, under a pitch-defining wire or string tie, over a small bridge resting on a snakeskin or wooden soundboard, to a string-holder at the bottom. In the Jiangnan region, strings are usually tuned a fifth apart (d' - a' for *erhu*). The bow stick is usually of bamboo, with its horsehair bow running between the pair of strings. An interesting, if apocryphal, story suggests that this unusual bow position was adopted by horseback-riding musicians of North China in order to prevent the bow being dropped while holding the reins. While *erhu* players today more commonly sit in chairs, the bow position has remained the same. *Huqin* varieties employed in Central and South China (some shown in Fig. 4.2) include: *erhu*, the lead Jiangnan fiddle, with (usually) a hexagonally shaped resonator covered with snakeskin; *erxian*, the lead Chaozhou fiddle, with small tubular resonator which rests on the bare toes of the upturned right foot (crossed over the left knee); *erxian*, the supporting Minnan fiddle, with relatively large tubular resonator covered with a thin soundboard of wood (Plate 16); *gaohu*, the lead Cantonese fiddle, somewhat smaller than the *erhu* and tuned a fourth or fifth higher, held with resonator between the player's knees (Plate 19); *yehu*, the medium-pitched supporting fiddle (Chaozhou and Cantonese), with resonator of coconut shell and a small seashell serving as a bridge. These types are held vertically, the sound chamber resting on the player's left thigh (except as noted above).[2]

The *zheng* multi-stringed zither is especially important within the Hakka and Chaozhou traditions (and on the Central Plain of North China as well), but is not a standard member of the other ensembles. Two basic construction styles are evident: the moderate-sized *zheng* of South China, with high arching soundboard and large wooden tuning pegs mounted diagonally on the soundboard itself—a construction method of Chaozhou makers in particular (Plate 20); and the larger northern style, with more moderate arching soundboard and small metal tuning pegs concealed at the end of the instrument (Plate 18 and Fig. 3.5). Strings on both

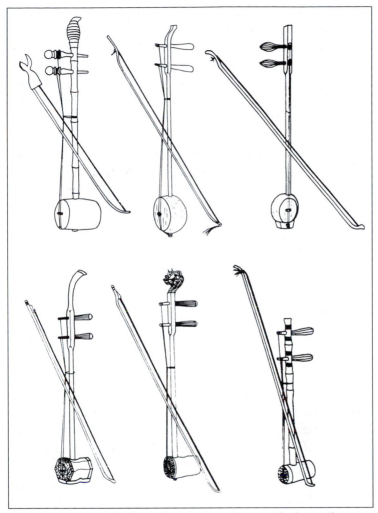

**4.2** *Sizhu* two-string fiddles, selected regional types. Clockwise (from upper left): *Erxian*, Minnan (*c*.82 cm); *Yehu*, Cantonese/Chaozhou (*c*.80 cm); *Banhu*, North China (*c*.70 cm); *Jinghu*, Beijing (*c*.50 cm); *Gaohu*, Cantonese (*c*.78 cm); *Erhu*, Jiangnan (*c*.80 cm). Contemporary line drawings.

are tuned to a pentatonic scale without half-steps (usually *sol-la-do-re-mi*) over a three-plus octave range. In today's practice, the instrument rests on a table or stand and is plucked with the right-hand fingernails or (most recently) with taped plastic finger picks. In performance, the left hand follows each string (to the left of its bridge) as it is plucked, applying alternating pressure for vibrato and pushing to obtain non-pentatonic pitches *fa* and *ti* and for various types of note bends. Capable of extraordinary tonal nuance, yet without requiring the great technical demands associated with the *pipa*, the *zheng* today is one of the most popular of the common-practice instruments.

## Supporting Stringed Instruments

Within the *sizhu* ensembles, some stringed instruments assume less significant roles, generally lending heterophonic support to the lead instruments. The *sanxian* lute, regularly employed in Jiangnan and Chaozhou music, is one such instrument. With long fretless neck of hardwood and small soundbox covered with snakeskin (Fig. 4.1), the *sanxian* has a tone colour somewhat similar to that of the Western banjo. Its three strings are tuned by any of several methods, commonly a fourth between lower and middle strings, and a fifth between middle and high strings (e.g. A - d - a). Three sizes are in use: large *sanxian*, for accompaniment of narrative song in North China; medium *sanxian*, used in Jiangnan *sizhu* and other traditions of Central-eastern China; and small *sanxian*, employed in Chaozhou music of South China. Roughly equivalent in Cantonese (and other) traditions is the *qinqin*, a lute with fretted neck and scalloped resonator covered with a wooden soundboard (Fig. 4.1 and Plate 19). These lutes are held in a horizontal (or diagonal) position, their soundboxes resting on the player's lap; they are plucked with fingernails or a small plectrum.

More active among the supporting strings is the *yangqin*, a struck dulcimer with two (or more) rows of bridges, and seven (or more) bridges in each row. Across each bridge run double- or triple-courses of metal strings, which are struck with two slender bamboo beaters. As seen in Fig. 4.1, the left row of bridges is positioned so as to divide the string lengths in a two-to-three relationship, thus enabling each course of strings to sound two pitches a fifth apart (utilizing both left and right sides). The right row of bridges, however, does not require exact positioning since only the left side is used (these for lower octave pitches). Older instruments were relatively small (with only two rows of seven bridges), the left and right ends of the soundboxes rounded, back edge jagged—hence the popular name *hudie qin* ('butterfly *qin*'). Since the 1950s, the *yangqin* has increased in size (with many more bridges and strings) and assumed a trapezoidal shape (Plate 19). This dulcimer is especially prevalent in the Jiangnan and Cantonese traditions (where its role often goes beyond mere accompaniment), and in Chaozhou music as well; it is less common in Hakka music, and absent from Minnan *nanyue*.

## Wind Instruments

The function of wind instruments in Chinese chamber music is both to maintain the (regional) pitch standard, and to provide timbral contrast against the dominant strings. Flutes, however, very often assume roles of melodic leadership. The *dizi* transverse bamboo flute is capable of especially colourful tonal characteristics. Located midway between the blowhole and group of six fingerholes is an extra hole, to be covered by a thin membrane of bamboo skin (*dimo*, which is peeled from the inside of the stalk). When properly adjusted, this membrane produces a vibrant and slightly 'buzzy' tone colour; and it amplifies the volume. Two size variants are usually acknowledged, the moderate-length *qudi* ('song flute'), which is one of the lead instruments in Jiangnan *sizhu* (Fig. 5.1), and the short flute *bangdi* of North China (Plate 24). The Jiangnan *qudi* is most commonly pitched in d"; the Cantonese flute is usually pitched one whole-step lower. Chaozhou music, however, is performed at a higher pitch, requiring a short flute similar to *bangdi* (commonly in f").[3] Good flute performance style requires adequate breath control and a basic knowledge of the lively idiomatic finger articulations.

The *xiao* vertical bamboo flute, with bevelled notch at the blowing end (but without the vibrating membrane), is pitched most commonly a fourth or fifth lower than the *dizi*, and has a less penetrating tone. The *xiao* is found in all *sizhu* ensembles, though several basic types are distinguished: the thin, long-internodal *zizhu xiao* ('purple bamboo *xiao*'), used in Jiangnan music and other traditions (Plates 17 and 18); the short, rather broad *dongxiao* ('open *xiao*') constructed from the root-end of bamboo, used in Minnan music (Plate 16); and the *yuping xiao* (named after the Yuping region of Guizhou province), a slender and often handsomely decorated flute, used primarily in solo performance.

The last wind instrument to be mentioned here is the *sheng* mouth organ. The *sheng* is usually held at an angle (to the player's right), the performer's right index finger inserted through the gap in the pipe circle to activate two inner fingerholes (Plate 21). Air is alternately exhaled and inhaled through the blowpipe (the acoustical process introduced in Chapter One). Most characteristic of traditional *sheng*

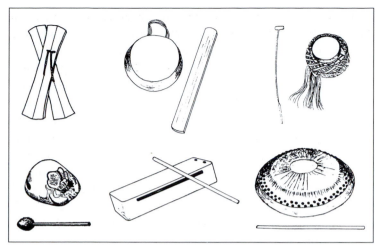

**4.3** *Sizhu* percussion, selected types. Clockwise (from upper left): *Paiban*, three-strip clapper (*c*.26 cm); *Jiaoluo*, Minnan flat-faced gong (diameter: *c.* 10 cm); *Xiangzhan*, Minnan small flat-faced gong suspended in a basket (diameter: *c*.6 cm); *Diangu*, Jiangnan flat drum with two heads (diameter: *c*.20 cm); *Nanbangzi*, Cantonese woodblock (*c*.24 cm); *Muyu* 'wooden fish' (width: *c*.10 cm or more). Contemporary line drawings.

performance is the rendering of melodies in continuous parallel fifths and octaves (seen in Fig. 4.4). While an important instrument in Jiangnan *sizhu* (and very widely employed in *chuida* ensemble types to the north), it is not employed at all in the more southern *sizhu* ensembles.

**Percussion**
Percussion instruments used in the chamber music traditions consist of just a few small idiophones and membranophones, their primary function being to maintain audible beats. Most notable amongst these is the *paiban* (Fig. 4.3), a clapper of three hardwood slabs suspended over the left thumb (by a connecting cord at the top end) and 'clapped' together at the

bottom. When the *paiban* is used in accompaniment of Beijing opera, the performer also strikes the thick-shelled 'single-skin drum' (*danpigu*) with a stick held in his right hand; when used in *sizhu* accompaniment, the performer alternately strikes a 'point drum' (*diangu*), a small relatively flat drum with two tacked heads (Fig. 4.3). In Minnan music, a five-slab Tang-style *paiban*, held between the two hands, marks principal beats in the same manner. In Cantonese music, a rectangular woodblock is used instead. Categorically known as *nanbangzi*, the Cantonese terms for woodblocks are onomatopoeic: *gok* (large block, Fig. 4.3), *duk* (medium block), and *dik* (small, high-pitched block).[4]

In some southern repertories (Cantonese and Minnan in particular), small bells, gongs, and other woodblocks are occasionally used as well. Most of these have been adopted from Buddhist ritual music where they are employed to accompany chant. Bells are generally small and hemispheric in contour, including: a small bell mounted on a stick, struck with a thin metal rod (*xing*); two small bells attached with a string and struck together (*pengling* or *shuangling*); and a medium-sized bell resting on a cushion and struck with a padded beater (*zuoqing*). Chamber music gong types are also small, such as the small flat-faced gongs employed in Minnan music (e.g. *xiangzhan* and *jiaoluo*, shown in Fig. 4.3) and, more occasionally, medium-sized changing-pitch gongs used in Cantonese music (q.v. Chapter Five). Most visually striking of this group of idiophones is the ubiquitous *muyu* ('wooden fish'), a partially hollowed woodblock in the abstract shape of a fish (Fig. 4.3), carved from a block of camphor (or other) wood and struck with a wooden beater. While *muyu* woodblocks used in chamber music are generally quite small (diameter: *c*.8–10 cm) and hand-held, instruments found in the old Buddhist temples are often large enough to require individual stands.

## Repertory and Style

The *sizhu* instrumental repertory is based upon a group of old tunes known as *qupai* ('named tunes'). The most popular and widespread of these is a melody known by several related names, notably *Baban* ('eight beat') in the Hakka and Chaozhou traditions (and in areas of North China), and *Liuban* ('six beat') in East China. Essential elements of this structure can be seen in the transcription of *Lao Liuban* (Fig. 4.4a), primary amongst them being the fixed number of beats (totalling sixty in this variant) and cadences emphasizing the pitches *sol* and *re* (occasionally *do*). The tune *Lao Liuban* is rarely performed by itself, though occasionally it is heard as a final section in a suite of pieces derived from it.

Over the last five hundred or so years, the *Liuban/Baban* model has been used repeatedly in the creation of new instrumental repertory. A short list of just a few of the most famous derived pieces would include 'Lofty Mountains and Flowing Waters' (*Gaoshan Liushui*) in the *zheng* repertory of Henan/Shandong provinces, 'Comfortable Breeze Melody' (*Xunfeng Qu*) and 'Emerging Lotus Blossoms' (*Chushui Lian*) in the Hakka/Chaozhou *zheng* repertory, 'White Snow in the Spring' (*Yangchun Baixue*) and 'Crazy Dance of the Golden Snake' (*Jinshe Kuangwu*) in the *pipa* repertory, and 'Palace Lantern Dance' (*Gongdeng Wu*) and 'Moderately-decorated Six-beat' (*Zhonghua Liuban*) in the Jiangnan *sizhu* repertory. While there are other pieces in these repertories derived from different (usually shorter) melodic models, those drawn from *Liuban/Baban* are always among the most highly revered in their respective areas.[5]

Pieces such as these have been derived by way of several traditional methods, notably through employment of modal shift (in which *ti* has been substituted for *la*, and *fa*

substituted for *mi*, creating a new modal feel to the old tune)
and by slowing the beat and interpolating melodic notes
(q.v. Thrasher 1989: 67–106). This last method, known as
'slow the tempo and add flowers' (*fangman jiahua*), has been
used in several ways. Most simply, it has served as the basis
for new instrumental pieces such as 'Palace Lantern Dance'
(*Gongdeng Wu*), a variant based upon *Lao Liuban* at less than

**4.4** *Lao Liuban* and *Zhonghua Liuban*, transcriptions.

half the speed of the original, together with the addition of melodic interpolations ('flowers'). The still slower *Liuban* variant known as 'Moderately decorated Six-beat' (*Zhonghua Liuban*, beginning shown in Fig. 4.4b) is approximately one-eighth the speed of the original, and characterized by greater rhythmic density in melodic interpolations. *Zhonghua Liuban* is a standard piece in the Jiangnan *sizhu* repertory.

The *sizhu* sound-ideal is best realized in ensembles without instrument duplication. A small Hakka ensemble, for example, might include one *xiao* and one *zheng* (Plate 18), possibly adding one *pipa* and one *huqin* if desired. Minnan ensembles are more standardized, almost always including one of each of the following: *xiao* (*dongxiao*), *huqin* (*erxian*), *pipa*, *sanxian*, and the five-slab *paiban* (Plate 16). Jiangnan ensembles, when performing in teahouse or music-club settings, are among the largest, usually (but not always) including one of each of the following: *dizi* and/or *xiao*, *sheng, huqin (erhu* and/or *zhonghu), pipa, sanxian, yangqin*, and *paiban/diangu* percussion (Plate 17). Cantonese ensembles also tend to be large, the essential instruments being *huqin* (*gaohu*) and *yangqin*, supported by *zhonghu* and/or the bass fiddle *dahu, qinqin*, or other lutes (sometimes including guitar-type lutes), small percussion, and wind instruments as diverse as *dizi, xiao, houguan* (reed pipe), and C-melody saxophone—but usually only one of each (Plate 19).

Sound-ideal is also manifest in the heterophonic texture of traditional music. Where other world cultures have developed complex harmonic and rhythmic systems, the Chinese system of melodic enrichment is based upon development of the various melodic parameters themselves. In traditional practice, when musicians perform the same basic melody simultaneously, they allow for the contrasting idiomatic characteristics of their respective instruments and interact with each other according to established performance principles. These heterophonic performance principles are based upon several factors, notably the distribution (among instruments) of melodic lines of varying rhythmic density and range. When lead instruments perform with high rhythmic density, supporting instruments simultaneously perform simpler 'variations'. As seen in the opening measures of *Zhonghua Liuban* (Fig. 4.4b), the *dizi* (flute) and *zhonghu* (tenor-range *erhu*) are most active in measure one, the *dizi* employing upper and lower finger articulations, the *zhonghu* employing portamenti (short on-the-beat slides on one string). The other instruments occupy supporting roles, the *sheng* performing notes of longer value in parallel fifths and octaves, the *pipa* and *yangqin* utilizing tremolos and octave pitch reiterations. The plucked strings become more active in measure two, the *dizi* again in measure three, and so forth. The essential element in traditional performance, and one that gives Chinese chamber music its richness and vibrancy, is the spontaneity with which such decisions are made. Good performers, playing without notation but with a thorough understanding of performance practice, improvise interactive 'variations'. As a result, every performance is different in textural detail.

The above principles of variation, then, taken together with the aesthetic values of the 'amateur ideal' introduced in Chapter Two (e.g. 'ancient and refined', 'covered and controlled'), form a nucleus of ideals in Chinese chamber music. But in the less conservative, large urban cultures of Shanghai and Hong Kong, more eclectic musicians found a nearly opposing ideal to be equally attractive—an ideal often explained with terms such as 'cheerful' (*huankuai*) and 'bustling' (*re'nao*). While clearly present in the upbeat

Jiangnan and Cantonese chamber musics, the 'cheerful' ideal is even more characteristic of the outdoor ceremonial ensembles. It is to these traditions, with their very colourful and loud wind and percussion instruments, that we now turn for a balanced perspective.

## Notes

1  For further discussion of these instruments, see Witzleben 1995: 37–57 and the individual entries in *The New Grove Dictionary of Musical Instruments* (Sadie 1984) or *The New Grove Dictionary of Music and Musicians*, 7th ed. (2000).

2  *Huqin* types employed in opera accompaniment throughout North China are equally diverse, including the diminutive Beijing opera fiddle *jinghu* (its stem and resonator of bamboo), *banhu* (similar to a small *yehu* but with laterally inserted pegs), *sihu* (four-string fiddle), and others.

3  The basic key on Chinese flutes is usually assigned to the pitch obtained by covering the upper three fingerholes (the bottom three holes left open).

4  More specialized among woodblock-type percussion is the pair of concussion sticks (*sibao*) used in Minnan chamber music, four rectangular slabs of bamboo which are struck together and shaken with highly choreographed arm movements.

5  One important exception is the *nanguan* repertory of southern Fujian and Taiwan, where other *qupai* tunes are more prominent.

# 5

## *Chuida* Instruments

THROUGHOUT HAN CHINA, there is another broad category of instrumental ensemble music that parallels and complements the string-and-flute oriented *sizhu* tradition—that is, the wind-and-percussion tradition. Since this type of music is widespread, each region possessing its own variants and terms, it will be identified here as *chuida* (literally 'blowing-hitting'). In fact, only a few wind-and-percussion traditions actually use this term, but it is nevertheless relatively well accepted as a music category and the term is a convenient counterpart to *sizhu*.

Ensembles of this type are led by any of several reed- or flute-type instruments, and nearly always supported by *sheng* and a variety of percussion instruments. *Chuida* music may generally be distinguished from *sizhu* music by several characteristics, most obviously in its reliance upon these louder wind-and-percussion instruments, but also in its association with traditional rituals such as funerals and calendrical ceremonies. In some areas of China, however, it is clear that *chuida* and *sizhu* repertories have influenced each other, most probably because these never-isolated traditions drew upon a common pool of *qupai* melodies, but also because local musicians in some areas (especially in South China) traditionally have performed both.

While *chuida*-type music is widespread, it is most characteristic of North China, where it dominates all other types of instrumental ensemble music. In southwestern Shandong province, the tradition known as *guchui* ('drumming-blowing') relies upon the shawm *suona* as its lead melody instrument, supported by *sheng* and various percussion (Plate 22). In central Hebei province (to the south of Beijing), one of several regional traditions is simply known as *yinyue* ('music'), for which the *guanzi* reed pipe serves as lead instrument, supported by *dizi*, *sheng*, *yunluo* (tuned gongs), and other percussion. A similar tradition is found in northern Shanxi province. Then, in and around the city of Xi'an (Shaanxi province, to the west of Shanxi), the reputedly ancient *guyue* ('drum music') is still preserved, a tradition relying primarily upon the *dizi* flute as lead instrument, supported by other winds and several types of drums.

Yet other local variants are prevalent in Central-eastern and South China, though these often include stringed instruments as well. For example, Sunan *chuida* of southern Jiangsu province utilizes the *dizi* (*qudi*) as lead instrument, supported by *sheng*, various stringed instruments, and percussion. In eastern Guangdong province, Chaozhou *daluogu* ('great gong-drum') relies upon the *suona* and short flute *xiaodi*, often supported by stringed instruments (but without *sheng*), together with a very large battery of gongs and drums. In Taiwan, their equivalent is locally known as *beiguan* ('northern pipe'), again with *suona* as lead instrument, supported by strings and percussion.[1]

## *Social Background*

Based upon visual evidence and early written accounts, ensembles playing reed pipes, transverse flutes, long horns, drums, and other instruments were already being employed in military processions by about the fifth century AD (Fig. 3.2). This early type of wind-and-percussion ensemble may have been influenced by practices in Central Asia and is believed to have been introduced by tribal peoples from

77

China's north, which helps explain its continuing dominance in this region. Similar ensemble types were employed over the centuries to accompany imperial processions (q.v. Chapter Three and Plate 15). During the fifteenth century, ensembles of Buddhist and Daoist musicians performed *chuida*-type music in the imperial court. Later dismissed, they continued performing in the local temples and for ritual observances of wealthy families in Beijing and other areas (q.v. Yang 1981: 987 ff.). This tradition remained strong into the mid-twentieth century, after which it was officially discouraged by the Chinese government as 'feudal superstition'. At present only a few temple ensembles are still functioning, the Guanghua (Buddhist) Temple ensemble in Beijing being one of the finest (Plate 23).

What is surprising is the survival of closely related ritual traditions in the hundreds of farming villages across North China, where today this music thrives. Villagers in China are mostly farmers by occupation—an unlikely population, one might think, in which to find the preservation of ancient instrumental traditions. But owing to their isolation from changing urban trends and government oversight, and indeed their very conservative nature, villagers maintain a rich calendar of rituals and festivals, notably rites of passage such as births, weddings, and funerals, and calendrical celebrations such as the lunar New Year. Among the life-cycle events, funerals receive more ritual attention than any other. Funerals in the villages are lengthy ceremonies, often lasting between one and several days, and requiring the services of Buddhist or Daoist priests (today usually performed by lay priests) and one or more music ensembles. Ensembles are comprised of male villagers, many of whom learned the tradition from their fathers and subsequently became ritual music specialists (q.v. Xue and Jones 1998: 21–33).

In central Hebei province and in districts to the south of Beijing, a funeral ceremony often begins with a colourful procession of musicians through the streets and dirt lanes, performing reed pipes or shawms, together with other wind instruments and percussion (Plate 24). In some villages, one or more performers on long valveless copper horns accompany the procession, playing long notes or overtone patterns to 'open the way' (*kaidao*). Upon arrival at the ritual site (formerly a local temple, today more normally a home), the musicians remain for performance during the ceremony itself. As throughout North China, the repertory performed during processions is known as 'processional music' (*xingyue*), while that performed at the ritual site is called 'sitting music' (*zuoyue*), since the musicians are then seated around a table.[2]

There are in fact two categories of ritual ensembles in the Hebei-Beijing area, a distinction based primarily upon the lead instrument used and its social status. Ensembles employing the *guanzi* reed pipe, sometimes called '*sheng-guan* ensembles' by scholars, are locally known as 'music associations' (*yinyue hui*). Ensembles employing the shawm-like *suona*, on the other hand, are commonly called 'blowing-drumming musicians' (*chuigu shou*). During performance, the former usually wear colourful robes (a sign of their ritual importance); the latter may simply wear street clothes. Indeed, 'music association' members hold themselves in a superior position to the 'blowing-drumming musicians'—which is not to suggest that the *suona* is any less popular because of this. In assessing this relationship, it must be remembered (from Chapter Three) that the reed pipe *guanzi* (historically known as *bili*) was an instrument of great significance in imperial court music of the Tang dynasty (618–907), whereas the more recently introduced *suona* was (and is) performed by lower-class professional musicians.[3]

## Instruments

The overall difference in instrumentation between *chuida* and *sizhu* ensembles is self evident. In some areas of China, however, this distinction is not sharp. As mentioned above, in Sunan *chuida*, stringed instruments are commonly used to accompany winds and percussion. And in Jiangnan *sizhu*, the *dizi* and *sheng* contribute timbral contrast to what is essentially a string ensemble. But throughout North China and along coastal Southeast China, these instrument groupings tend to remain separate.

**Melody Instruments**
Wind instruments dominate *chuida* music, though very often sets of tuned gongs (*yunluo*) are also employed for timbral contrast. Most significant among the northern wind instruments is the *guanzi*. The *guanzi* is essentially a reed pipe, a short cylindrical wooden tube, with an oversized double reed mounted in the blowing end (Fig. 5.1 and Plate 23). The instrument has seven frontal fingerholes and one thumbhole. Sizes differ between regions, and even within regions, the most common type in Hebei province producing e' as its lowest pitch. As seen in Chapter Three, the *guanzi* emerged from the historic *bili*. This older bamboo reed pipe had a second thumbhole at the back, which later was found to be unnecessary in common-practice music and it was eliminated.[4] Reed pipes used in North China today are made of hardwood, inlaid at both ends with metal rings to control

80

cracking. Within village and temple *sheng-guan* ensembles, the *guanzi* has retained its position as principal lead instrument.

The *suona*, while of lower social status in North China than the *guanzi*, is considerably more popular throughout the various regions of the country. The name *suona* (q.v. Chapter Three) is considered something of an academic term. Among performing musicians the instrument is known by local names such as *dadi*, *laba*, and others. Sizes differ from one region to another, the smallest variant known as *haidi*. The shawm-like *suona* tube is constructed from a redwood or other hardwood. It has a conical bore (unlike the cylindrical *guanzi*), and seven fingerholes plus one thumbhole. A very small double reed is inserted at the blowing end, the lower end extended by a large flaring metal bell (Fig. 5.1 and Plate 22). In performance, the player's mouth completely encloses the reed (without touching it) and he very commonly utilizes circular breathing in production of a continuous melodic flow.[5]

The two other wind instruments of importance in northern music are *dizi* and *sheng* (Fig. 5.1). Already introduced within the context of the Jiangnan *sizhu* ensemble (q.v. Chapter Four), the flutes and mouth organs employed in the ensembles of North China reflect some small differences in construction and usage. The northern *dizi*, generally known as *bangdi* (Plate 24), is shorter in length than the Jiangnan *qudi* flute, and pitched between a major second and perfect fourth higher (commonly e″, f″, or g″, the upper three holes covered). Performance techniques on the *bangdi* tend to be more animated, including a variety of distinctive finger and tonguing techniques. When performing in the *sheng-guan* ensembles, however, the flute generally assumes a role of support. The northern *sheng* resembles

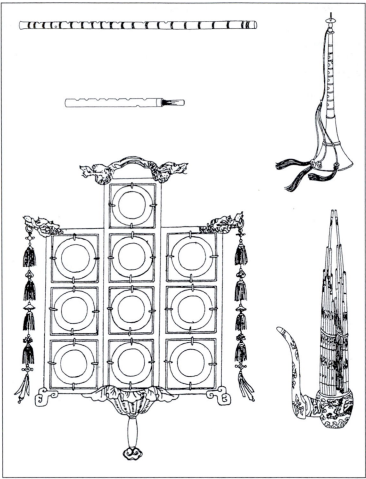

**5.1** *Chuida* wind instruments and *yunluo*. Clockwise (from upper left): *Qudi*, transverse flute with six fingerholes (*c*.40–60 cm); *Suona* (marked 'jinkoujiao') shawm with eight fingerholes (reed not shown) (*c*.45 cm); *Sheng*, mouth organ with detachable blowpipe (*c*.50 cm); *Yunluo* ('cloud gongs'), frame of ten gongs (gong diameter: *c*.10 cm); *Guanzi*, reed pipe with large double reed, eight fingerholes (*c*.18 cm or more). Drawings from *Lülü Zhengyi* (1713).

the Jiangnan *sheng* in external appearance but, like the flute, it is pitched higher. It also plays a more active role within ensembles (compared to the Jiangnan *sheng*) and, as a result, windchests tend to be large for greater volume (Plate 22). Seventeen pipes are standard for most traditional instruments, though generally only fourteen (or fewer) have reeds.

Visually most distinctive among northern melody instruments is the *yunluo* ('cloud gongs'), a set of ten (or more) vertically suspended small gongs in a portable frame (Fig. 5.1). These are struck with a tipped beater. The usage of this instrument in imperial processions and religious functions from the fourteenth century onward has been mentioned in Chapter Three (Plates 15 and 24). *Yunluo* gongs are basin shaped and all of the same diameter but varying in thickness (thicker gongs vibrating at higher pitches). They are pitched diatonically over the range of an octave and a third (commonly with a″ as the lowest pitch). In performance, the rhythmic effect of emphasizing melodic afterbeats adds an essential element to the overall musical texture.

**Percussion Instruments**

Percussion instruments employed in the ritual ensembles are of four general types: cymbals, gongs, drums, and woodblocks (or clappers). Many (but not all) have onomatopoeic names, such as *bo* and *cha* (cymbal types), *dangdang* (or *dangzi*, small gong), *gongluo* (large gong), and *bangzi* (woodblocks). Unlike the light percussion used in the chamber traditions (which principally serve to mark beats), the louder cymbals, gongs, and drums used in ritual ensembles play a more active role in rhythmic interactions with the other instruments and performance of percussion interludes.

Cymbals and gongs are constructed of 'resonant copper' (*xiangtong*), an alloy of three or more parts of copper to one part of tin. Cymbals (in pairs) issue their greatest resonance at their rims, gongs at their centres. While there are many different local names for cymbals, two broad sub-types are usually distinguished: *bo*, with a pronounced hemispheric bulb occupying the entire middle half of its surface, through which a strip of cloth is tied for holding (Fig. 5.2); and the generally larger *nao*, flatter in shape and of thinner metal, with a small central knob which itself is held during performance. Gongs used in North China are also of several kinds, notably the historic medium-sized *dangzi*, a flat-faced gong suspended in an L-shaped frame (Plate 15); and *daluo* ('large gong') (Fig. 5.2) and *xiaoluo* ('small gong'), somewhat larger gongs with curved profiles and flat central striking areas. Most characteristic of these gongs is the fact that their pitches change after being struck, that of the *daluo* descending, the *xiaoluo* pitch ascending. As with most percussion instruments, specific names vary from one region to another.[6]

The various drums differ not so much in construction as in size. Most drums in use today are barrel-shaped, their two heads tacked into wooden shells (similar to construction methods used for the ancient ritual drums discussed in Chapter One). Large drums of variable size resting in a frame are appropriately called *dagu* ('large drum', diameter: *c*.50 cm or more, Plate 15); medium-sized drums are commonly called *tanggu* ('hall drum', Fig. 5.2). Other related sub-types are employed as well.[7] Drums are used primarily in 'sitting music', especially prevalent in Xi'an *guyue*. In some regional traditions, a pair of short, round concussion bars known as *bangzi* are used to maintain beats. *Bangzi* are constructed from a resonant hardwood, one thick bar (held in the left hand) and one thin bar which is struck against it.

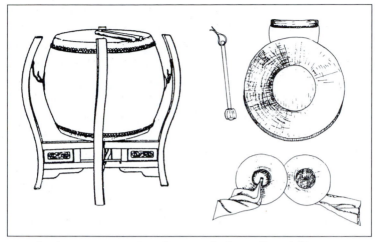

**5.2** *Chuida* percussion, selected types. Clockwise (from left): *Tanggu*, medium-sized barrel-drum in stand (diameter: *c*.25 cm or more); *Daluo* ('large gong') and padded beater (diameter: *c*.25 cm or more); *Bo* (*tongbo*), small cymbals (diameter: *c*.15 cm or more). Contemporary line drawings.

## Horns

End-blown valveless copper horns of various shapes have been used in Chinese military and ritual processions for close to two thousand years. While the earliest horns appear to have been curved (Fig. 3.2), by the Ming dynasty at least two other styles had emerged: *laba* ('Lama horn'), a thin straight trumpet-like instrument with flaring bell, and *haotong* ('signal tube'), also straight but with very large tubular bell.[8] These horns are usually constructed of several collapsing sections of tubing (with rounded bulbs at each joint), extended lengths reaching 100 cm or more. At the blowing end is a hemispheric cup mouthpiece with flattened rim. Horns are still used in outdoor processions to announce auspicious events.

85

## *Repertory and Style*

'Processional music' in North China is comprised entirely of short tunes (*xiaoqu*). These are performed at moderate tempo (in accompaniment of processions) and connected by percussion interludes. Some tunes such as 'Grazing the Donkey' (*Fanglü*) are unique to the region; others include widely known *qupai* tunes such as 'Many Years of Happiness' (*Wannian Huan*) and 'Eight-beat' (*Baban*, q.v. Chapter Four). 'Sitting music', on the other hand, is most commonly organized in an extended suite of melodies, some specifically religious in origin. Suite organization is quite similar throughout North China, beginning with a slow, free-metered prelude, followed by a longer main section of several or more melodies successively performed at slow, moderate, and fast tempos, and concluding with a short coda. All melodies are connected by percussion interludes.

While some stylistic elements are similar to *sizhu* music (e.g. a few shared melodies, pentatonic structures, heterophonic textures), the *sheng-guan* sound-ideal and aesthetic are quite different. Whereas *sizhu* ensembles are generally small in size, comprised of relatively soft instruments with one instrument per part, the *sheng-guan* sound-ideal requires a large ensemble (commonly ten to twelve musicians) and a continuous flood of sound, all melody instruments (ideally) doubled for maximum strength. The celebratory effect is quite glorious.

# Notes

1   Most of these regional traditions are introduced in the Chinese-language studies by Gao Houyong (1981) and Yuan Jingfang (1987), and in the West by Stephen Jones (1995), where a more comprehensive bibliography can be found.

2   While this division is a notable characteristic of North China, it must be pointed out that South China also has 'sitting music' (though usually performed on *sizhu* instruments), and 'processional music' (played by *suona* bands).

3   Specific association of the *suona* with lower-class values, however, is not apparent in all areas of China. In rural Taiwan, for example, where neither the *guanzi* nor the *sheng* is performed, processional funeral ensembles rely entirely upon the *suona* (in multiple numbers) to carry the melodies. And in Shandong province (northeastern China), the *suona* is often considered something of an art instrument (with a highly developed repertory). So, it is evident that associations between instruments and status are based upon regional beliefs, absence of other prestigious instruments, and readings of history.

4   Some old instruments in usage today still have both thumbholes, the lower one permanently plugged. Reed pipes of bamboo, known as *houguan* (with seven fingerholes and a single thumbhole), are still employed in Cantonese ensembles.

5   In circular breathing, players continuously exhale by periodically closing the back of their throats and using their cheeks to force out reserve air while inhaling through the nose.

6   In South China and Taiwan, other gong sub-types are more common, notably: *douluo*, *shenbo*, and other quite large flat-faced gongs with broad turned-back shoulders (between 40–80 cm in diameter); and large *gongluo* or *mangluo* gongs with raised knobs in their centres (similar to the Javanese *kempul*).

7   The *zhangu* ('war drum') is smaller and sounds a higher pitch. The relatively narrow *yaogu* ('waist drum', not to be confused with the Tang-style hourglass drum of the same name), is suspended by a strap from the neck of the performer and used in dance-song accompaniment (but not in *chuida* music).

8   Other names are used as well to identify these horn types. On the southeast coast of China and in Taiwan, *laba* with curved-back bells and end-blown water buffalo horns (*niujiao hao*) are also employed within ritual contexts.

# Postscript:
## Twentieth-Century Developments

THROUGHOUT THE NINETEENTH century, traditional Chinese government and ideology took one heavy hit after another— the Opium Wars, the Taiping Rebellion, one-sided trade relations with the Western world, and general corruption in the Qing government. Soon after the turn of the twentieth century, Chinese leaders and writers realized that if China were to deal with Western powers on an equal basis, it must start adopting Western ways. By the mid-1930s, the imperial examination system had been abandoned, the classical language replaced by a more accessible idiom, and the annual sacrifices to Confucius discontinued. Increasing numbers of university students had left to study abroad.

Every aspect of Chinese culture was touched in one way or another by these changes. With a view towards making music more accessible to the common people, traditional ideals thought to be elitist were replaced by more dramatic and immediately attractive styles, such as use of brighter tone colours, orchestrated arrangements with rudimentary harmonies, and Western forms. Indeed, these changes were increasingly required in performance of the newly emergent concert-hall music, *guoyue* ('national music'), the composed music of the young and restless students coming out of the music conservatories.

During the 1950s, a Russian-influenced movement to 'improve' the musical instruments became something of a national goal. In the instrument factories of Shanghai, Suzhou, and Beijing, the ranges, temperaments, and volumes of all *guoyue* instruments were altered to accommodate the new ideal. On the *erhu*, strings were changed from silk to steel, and placed under greater tension, its bow fitted with an end screw so that bow-hair tension could be adjusted (as on the Western violin bow). The new *pipa* was similarly given metal strings, and frets were positioned to produce half-steps for performance in keys formerly never needed. On both instruments, playing range was increased from one-and-a-half or two octaves to three or four octaves. In addition, sound chambers were enlarged to produce the volumes required within the new concert halls, a change especially noticeable in *zheng* and *yangqin* construction, where frames were nearly doubled in size. Additional strings were added as well—*zheng* strings increased from sixteen to eighteen or twenty-one— and bridges on the *yangqin* increased from two rows to three or four.

Flutes were similarly affected, though mostly in terms of temperament. On the older *dizi* and *xiao*, fingerholes had been placed at roughly equal distance, thereby producing mixed small-whole-step and three-quarter-step intervals. Defenders of the old practice recognized this flute temperament as having great value in that it allowed for performance in all seven 'keys' (*diao*) and, when performed together with instruments tuned in other temperaments (such as *sheng* or *pipa*), it created a natural system of consonance and dissonance without the need for leading tones. When I recently discussed the traditional flute temperament with a Chinese instrument designer who was active during this period, his dismissive response was 'well, we solved that problem back in the '50s'. Indeed they did, initially with an eleven-hole equal-tempered *dizi* (requiring the use of both fingertips and various inner finger joints), and subsequently with a more practical six-hole flute with hole positions adjusted to produce tempered whole-steps and half-steps. The eleven-hole flute is now a museum piece, but the six-hole tempered *dizi* is presently the only transverse flute used in concert-hall performances. It is commonly made in several different keys. The *sheng* mouth organ, on the other hand, had been tuned to pure whole- and half-steps since about the eighth century, and probably much earlier. As a result, *sheng* temperament remained unchanged, but windchests were enlarged and made increasingly of nickel-plated brass (rather than wood). Many new *sheng* designs also emerged, requiring additional pipes, use of accordion key technology to activate the reeds, and other inventions.

Because this new concert-hall tradition was modelled so completely on the Western symphonic ideal, instruments were built in families of soprano, alto, tenor, and bass, and ensemble sizes grew to between about three and ten times the size of traditional Jiangnan or Cantonese ensembles. Contemporary Chinese orchestras today usually include one or two high-pitched *banhu* or *gaohu* fiddles, a good number of *erhu* fiddles, and a smaller number of alto-range *zhonghu* and tenor- and bass-range *dahu* fiddles (often together with cellos and double basses as well). Among plucked and struck strings, the basic instruments are *pipa* lutes, high-pitched *pipa*-like *liuyeqin* lutes, *yangqin* dulcimers, and the revived *ruan* lutes in several size variants, notably the tenor-range *zhongruan* and bass-range *daruan*. *Zheng* zithers are also occasionally used. Wind instruments usually include *dizi* flutes (in two or more sizes), *sheng* mouth organs (frequently in several size variants), sometimes *guanzi* or *suona*, and a wide range of Chinese and Western percussion instruments.

In today's world, the older instrumental traditions survive with remarkable integrity, but they tend to be hidden along the back lanes, in the clubs and temples, most practitioners belonging to the older generation. Performances of traditional chamber music are rarely heard in concert halls, whose stages are dominated by young conservatory-trained musicians, virtuosos who prefer the newly composed *guoyue* repertory and (very occasionally) special arrangements of traditional music. Exciting and intoxicating as this new concert-hall music is, it is unfortunate that, for Western (and even urban Chinese) audiences, this tradition is usually the only 'Chinese music' they may ever hear.

# Selected Bibliography

Cao Zheng (1983), 'A Discussion of the History of the Gu Zheng', *Asian Music*, 14(2): 1–16.

Cheng Deh-yuan (1984), *Zhongguo Yueqi Xue* (Study of Chinese Musical Instruments), Taipei: Shengyun.

Cheung Sai-bung (1974–5), *Zhongguo Yinyue Shilun Shugao* (Historical Studies of Chinese Music), 2 vols. Hong Kong: Union Press.

Chuang Pen-li (1963), *Zhongguo Gudai zhi Paixiao* (Panpipes of Ancient China), Taipei: Academia Sinica [Eng. summary].

DeWoskin, Kenneth (1982), *A Song for One or Two: Music and the Concept of Art in Early China*, Ann Arbor: University of Michigan.

Fontein, J. and Tung Wu (1973), *Unearthing China's Past*, Boston: Museum of Fine Arts.

Gao Houyong (1981), *Minzu Qiyue Gailun* (Outline of National Instrumental Music), Nanjing: Jiangsu Renmin.

Gulik, Robert van (1940), *The Lore of the Chinese Lute: an Essay in Ch'in Ideology*, Tokyo: Sophia University Press.

Han Kuo-huang (1979), 'The Modern Chinese Orchestra', *Asian Music*, 11(1): 1–40.

——— (1991), *Zhongguo Yueqi Xunli* (A Tour of Chinese Musical Instruments), Taipei: Wenjianhui.

Hayashi Kenzō (1962), *Dongya Yueqi Kao* (Examination of East Asian Instruments), Beijing: Yinyue [trans. from Japanese] (Hong Kong rpt. 1972).

Hayashi Kenzō et al. (1967), *Shōsōin no Gakki* (Musical Instruments in the Shōsōin). Tokyo: Nihon Keizai Shimbun Sha [Eng. summary].

Jones, Stephen (1995), *Folk Music of China: Living Instrumental Traditions*, Oxford: Clarendon Press; 1998 rpt. with CD.

Kishibe, Shigeo (1960–1), *Tōdai Ongaku no Rekishi-teki Kenkyū* (Historic Study of the Music in the Tang Dynasty), ii, Tokyo [Eng. summary].

Kuttner, Fritz (1990), *The Archaeology of Music in Ancient China*, New York: Paragon.

Lee Yuan-yuan and Shen Sin-yan (1999), *Chinese Musical Instruments*, Chicago: Chinese Music Society of North America.

Li Chunyi (1996), *Zhongguo Shanggu Chutu Yueqi Zonglun* (Synthesized Essays on Ancient Unearthed Musical Instruments in China), Beijing: Wenwu.

Liang Mingyue (1972), *The Chinese Ch'in: Its History and Music*, Taipei: Chinese Music Association.

——— (1985), *Music of the Billion: An Introduction to Chinese Musical Culture*, New York: Heinrichshofen.

Liu Dongsheng et al., ed. (1987), *Zhongguo Yueqi Tuzhi* (Pictorial Record of Chinese Musical Instruments), Beijing: Qinggongye.

Liu Dongsheng and Yuan Quanyou, ed. (1988), *Zhongguo Yinyue Shi Tujian* (Pictorial Guide to Chinese Music History), Beijing: Renmin Yinyue.

Liu Dongsheng, ed. (1992), *Zhongguo Yueqi Tujian* (Pictorial Guide to Chinese Musical Instruments), Ji'nan: Shandong Jiaoyu.

Lui Tsun-yuen (1968), 'A Short Guide to Ch'in', *Selected Reports*, 1(2): 179–204.

Mok, Robert (1978), 'Ancient Musical Instruments Unearthed in 1972 from the Number One Han Tomb at Ma Wang Tui, Changsha', *Asian Music*, 10(1): 39–91.

Moule, A.C., (1908), 'A List of the Musical and Other Sound Producing Instruments of the Chinese', *Journal of the Royal Asiatic Society, North China Branch*, 39: 1–160.

Myers, John (1992), *The Way of the Pipa*, Kent: Kent State University Press.

Picken, Laurence (1969), 'T'ang Music and Musical Instruments', *Toung Pao*, LV: 74–122.

Sadie, Stanley, ed. (1984), *The New Grove Dictionary of Musical Instruments*, 3 vols., London: Macmillan.

Shen Sin-yan (1986), 'The Acoustics of *Bianzhong* Bell Chimes of China', *Chinese Music*, 9(3): 53–7; cont. in 1987 issues.

So, Jenny F., ed. (2000), *Music in the Age of Confucius*, Washington, D.C.: Smithsonian Institution.

Stock, Jonathan (1993), 'A Historical Account of the Chinese Two-stringed Fiddle', *The Galpin Society Journal*, 46: 83–113.

Thrasher, Alan R., (1989), 'Structural Continuity in Chinese *Sizhu*: the *Baban* Model', *Asian Music*, 20(2): 67–106.

———— (1993), '*Bianzou*: Performance Variation Techniques in Jiangnan *Sizhu*', *CHIME Journal*, 6: 4–20.

———— (1996), 'The Chinese Sheng: Emblem of the Phoenix', *ACMR Reports*, 9(1): 1–20.

Tong Kin-woon (T'ang Chien-yüan) (1973), *Ch'in-fu*, 3 vols., Taipei: Lianguan.

———— (1983), *Shang Musical Instruments* (diss., Wesleyan University); rpt. in *Asian Music*, 14(2) and 15(1) (1983), and 15(2) (1984).

Von Falkenhausen, Lothar (1993), *Suspended Music: Chimebells in the Culture of Bronze Age China*, Berkeley: University of California Press.

Witzleben, J. Lawrence (1995), '*Silk and Bamboo' Music in Shanghai*, Kent: Kent State University Press.

Xue Yibing and Jones, Stephen (1998), 'The Music Associations of Hebei Province', in *Musical Performance: Tradition and Change in the Performance of Chinese Music*, 2(1): 21–33.

Yang Mu (1993), *Chinese Musical Instruments*, Canberra; incl. cassettes.

Yang Yinliu (1981), *Zhongguo Gudai Yinyue Shigao* (Draft History of Ancient Chinese Music), 2 vols., Beijing: Renmin Yinyue.

Yuan Bingchang and Mao Jizeng, ed. (1986), *Zhongguo Shaoshu Minzu Yueqi Zhi* (Dictionary of Musical Instruments of the Chinese Minorities), Beijing: Xin Shijie.

Yuan Jingfang (1987), *Minzu qiyue* (National Instrumental Music), Beijing: Renmin Yinyue.

Zhao Feng, ed. (1992), *Zhongguo Yueqi: China Supplementary Volume I, Instruments*, Hong Kong: Zhuhai [Eng. summary].

Zheng Ruzhong (1993), 'Musical Instruments in the Wall Paintings of Dunhuang', *CHIME Journal*, 7: 4–56 [trans. A. Schimmelpenninck].

*Zhongguo Yinyue Shi Cankao Tupian* (Chinese Music History in Reference Pictures) (1964) vol. 9, ed. by the Music Research Institute, Beijing: Yinyue.

*Zhongguo Yinyue Wenwu Daxi* (Compendium of Chinese Musical Relics), (1996–), multi-volume series, ed. by the Music Research Institute, Zhengzhou: Daxiang.

# Index